STEVE BRIA
ment professio
community care, reiugee resettlement and organization development. He has twenty years' international experience of advising and educating managers from top companies, government and voluntary groups, and his specializations include negotiation skills, partnership development and service improvement, especially in health care. He is the author of *Working It Out* (Russell House, 2002) and is a founding member of the Association for Social Development. He lives in Sussex with his family.

THE MYSTERY OF MEETING

MEETING

Relationships as a Path of Discovery

Steve Briault

with drawings by Gill David

Sophia Books

Sophia Books
Hillside House, The Square
Forest Row, East Sussex
RH18 5ES

www.rudolfsteinerpress.com

Published by Sophia Books 2010
An imprint of Rudolf Steiner Press

A catalogue record for this book is available from the British Library

ISBN 978 1 85584 233 5

Cover by Andrew Morgan Design
Typeset by DP Photosetting, Neath, West Glamorgan
Printed and bound in Great Britain by Cromwell Press Group

For:

Anthea, sister across the threshold, who warmed my childhood; and Phoebe, sister to my sons, in celebration of all we are learning from each other.

Contents

In the strictest sense, all geniune morality depends upon this ability to enter with one's own soul into the soul of another . . . without which no true social order amongst people on earth can be maintained.

Rudolf Steiner

Why I wrote this book

Glancing through a friend's bookcase some years ago, I was struck by seeing so many books on relationships—how to love, how to be loved, how to avoid loving too much (whatever that means), how to survive divorce, how to understand the other sex, how to create intimacy, how to overcome the fear of intimacy, how to be a step-parent, how to use anger constructively, how to get what you want, how to be a sibling without rivalry, how to rescue your relationship . . . all full of good advice, no doubt, but something central seemed missing.

Two things stood out clearly. Firstly, that people living today are hugely focused on how we relate with one another; while also being hugely challenged by the breakdown in traditional relationship structures such as marriage and community. Secondly, and my main incentive in writing this book, is that none of these texts seemed really to address the inner aspect of relationships. They did not seem to recognize the central reality which I will try to describe in what follows, which is that *the encounter with another person is a threshold-experience*. By this I mean that each person is an unknown world, and between us there is an opening, a doorway we might step through. When we meet someone—especially in profound, intense ways—we are confronted with experiences, either real or potential, that challenge our sense of self.

Our relationships—with our family, colleagues, friends, lovers, partners—are decisive factors in our lives. More than outer success, wealth or fame, they make the difference between joy and sorrow, development and stagnation, fulfilment and frustration. They stimulate and require us to reflect on our own initiatives and reactions. They lead us to thresholds of emotion and discovery. If we can navigate these thresholds with our eyes open, relationships can be a path for a kind of initiation, taking us beyond our self-centred isolation into new and inspiring worlds of experience.

I would like to make clear that I make no claim to being an expert on relationships; still less to having discovered any universal solutions to the issues and challenges with which our relationships confront us. In fact, I would be highly sceptical of any such claims. So this book will not offer the kind of success stories about the author's marriage, family life, friendships or business which many self-help handbooks provide. What I can say is that the complex, baffling struggle to build and sustain constructive relationships is a central life-theme for me; that I have striven to learn as much as possible from my mistakes—which unfortunately does not always preclude repeating them—and that the book contains insights and perspectives which I have acquired (mostly from others) and found enlightening and helpful. I hope readers may find some similar benefits.

I

MEETING OUR THRESHOLDS

1. Thresholds and Individuation

A first proposition:
Behind the tensions in national and global society today lies a basic, existential tension between individualism and group identification.

We live in an age when things are falling apart. With exponential speed, structures that have supported us for generations, millennia, are dissolving: families, the class system, traditional communities. Old career structures are disappearing, the bond between employers and employees is shifting. With so many things changing that people have counted on for support and meaning in their lives, the strain is showing. Stress levels are high; addiction a near-epidemic; we have become familiar with isolation and antisocial behaviour. At the same time, all around we can see people searching for identity. The pseudo-tribalism of gangs, racist violence, xenophobia, sects, fundamentalist movements, can all be seen as symptoms of people needing to feel a sense of belonging.

The tension between being free and needing to belong plays itself out in every household, classroom and workplace. Most of us do not like being told what to believe, how to behave, what to read or listen to, what to watch, wear or eat. We want to make our own choices—especially in who we relate to and how. But this personal freedom comes at a cost—an isolation which consumption and entertainment cannot fill. We want to be free individuals, *and* to feel a sense of connectedness with others. We want autonomy, and *also* to be part of a community that supports us and gives a sense of wider identity.

As individuals, we can try to solve this, in part, by picking and choosing what we belong to. We might leave behind our parents' religions, our local roots, or rules that were forced on us. We can choose others that appeal or make more sense. We can select our own friends, family, our own religious movement. We can identify with anything from a football team or a pub, to a sailing club or knitting circle: there are thousands of possible communities that we could join, to reflect who we are and want to be. If we are lucky, we feel a sense of belonging in our work and in a community of colleagues.

On the national level, state-run welfare structures have tried to replace the 'natural' sense of mutual responsibility which was present in traditional communities. In many countries, however, these systems seem to have reached their limits and are now increasingly being rolled back— leaving people wondering what forms or arrangements could support both self-responsibility and social inclusive-ness. On an even wider level, globalization brings both threats and opportunities for individuals, in a massive acceleration of the ongoing transition from a 'power-based society' to a 'bargaining society'. The search for new forms of community, from co-ops to communes, was an important theme in the later part of the twentieth century.

But communities, including self-chosen ones, bring their own problems: friends drift away, families split up, religion or sport brings us into conflict with people who have competing allegiances. Job-hopping or redundancy separates colleagues. Sooner or later, we find ourselves more alone than we want to be, or more restricted than we had expected by our relationships. We are confronted by the two major issues of social groupings:

- managing the boundaries between our own and other groups; and
- the loss of individual freedom.

Every social context creates insiders and outsiders: to a greater or lesser extent, it divides the group from others as well as uniting the individuals within it. Communities have boundaries to manage, borders to protect, beliefs and symbols to uphold, claims to promote and identities to sustain. All too often, this leads not only to healthy competition, but to conflict with other groups, from territorial struggles, organizational or family feuds, sectarianism, nationalism, through to terrorism and reprisal.

> In the rear window of the car in front at the traffic lights, a sticker represents a football player, in red kit, urinating on a blue sports sweater, and grinning. On the shirt of the urinator is the word 'United'; on the blue shirt 'City'. What are the forces which make such an image attractive for the driver to display? Why does the enmity between teams from the same town create such powerful emotions? Is this a game, a form of playful teasing, or are deeper and stronger impulses driving such strong and apparently arbitrary tribalism?

Within communities too, there are usually tensions. We no longer automatically respect those in leadership roles; people want scope for personal initiative, and demand resources to help them express it. People strive for consensus, but it often eludes them. Competition inside a community threatens its ability to stay together, leading to factionalism and fractures.

Individuation

Perhaps we need to see these contradictory tendencies—the urge to exercise free personal choice on the one hand, and the desire to identify with a wider community on the other— as expressions of an important social evolution. The process of *individuation* is both result and cause of all this tension. It brings an increasing demand and potential for personal autonomy, but also insecurity and isolation.

The philosopher Rudolf Steiner formulated what he called the 'basic sociological law' which expresses an archetypal development process that we can observe in communities of all kinds and on every scale, from a family or a business to an entire civilization. It runs as follows:

> In the early stages of cultural development, human beings strive to create social groupings; initially, the interests of the individual are sacrificed to the interests of these groups. Further development, however, leads to the emancipation of the individual from the interests of the group, and to the free unfolding of the needs and strengths of single human beings.[1]

If Steiner is right that such a pattern is a universal tendency, this 'law' has far-reaching implications for community-building of all kinds. It means that the kinds of sacrifices which people will freely make during the early 'pioneering' phase[2] of an institution, a business, a revolutionary state, or a marriage, cannot be expected to continue. The community will only continue to be healthy and successful if it takes

---

[1] Rudolf Steiner, *Gesammelte Aufsätze zur Kultur-und Zeitgeschichte*, GA 31.
[2] See B. Lievegoed, *The Developing Organization*, Blackwell, 1991.

account of this individualizing process, allows for and supports it. Countless leaders, entrepreneurs, founders and spouses have paid the price, along with their followers and partners, of ignoring this law.

This leads to a second proposition:
We need to embrace individuation as an evolutionary necessity; it is counterproductive to resist or try to reverse it. The challenge is to develop an 'ethical individualism' which can create healthy relationships between increasingly self-directed human beings.

This challenge leads us to meet *thresholds*, boundaries of awareness, comfort and competence, in new, intensified, and unpredictable ways. We meet these boundaries in our experience of the world, in ourselves, and with others. So the central question which this book attempts to address is:

What is the nature of the thresholds we encounter in our social, personal and professional relationships; and how can these be met and managed in constructive, developmental ways?

2. Three Thresholds

The first night of the holiday: a mother is putting her child to bed. The child is tired but excited, won't settle, can't let go of the day. Fretful and clingy, he demands one story or song after another, and keeps finding more things to want, caught in the cycle of needing his mother's attention; separation anxiety. The mother needs to be free of the child—to focus, rest, have time to feel herself. Finally, being imprisoned in the cot brings security after brief distress: the mother goes downstairs, the child cries then accepts and sleeps. A small threshold has been crossed, for both of them.

What is a threshold?

In this book, the term 'threshold' will be used to mean a *boundary between different modes of consciousness*. The boundary between waking and sleeping is an obvious example—one which we all cross in both directions regularly and often unreflectingly. Even these transitions, however familiar, can be problematic: sometimes it is hard to get to sleep, sometimes hard to wake up. Experiences may be carried over this threshold, and perhaps transformed on the way. We may awaken with new ideas, changed attitudes, or fresh resolves, out of the night. The intermediate state we call dreaming has its own more subtle thresholds in both directions—towards waking consciousness, where we may momentarily become confused about which 'reality' we are in, and towards deep sleep, from which conscious impressions can rarely be retrieved, but where important processes nevertheless seem to take place in our psyche.

A far more mysterious and challenging threshold, of course, lies at the final boundary of each of our biographies. Human culture has been constantly permeated with a rich variety of images, myths, stories, doctrines and speculation about what lies beyond death. Whatever the notional materialism of recent scientific culture may say, or whatever its reluctance to say anything, indeed, most of us find it hard simply to dismiss as meaningless the question which Hamlet articulated, and which held him back from suicide:

> . . . who would . . . grunt and sweat under a weary life,
> But that the dread of something after death,
> The undiscover'd country from whose bourn
> No traveller returns, puzzles the will,
> And makes us rather bear those ills we have
> Than fly to others that we know not of?[3]

How do we live with the awareness of the inevitability of death? In Western culture, the most popular approaches seem to be either to avoid thinking and talking about it altogether, or to adopt a religious doctrine which offers reassurance of a blissful continuation or transformation of consciousness after death, in return for piety and morality in earthly life. Perhaps not surprisingly, the second strategy seems to become more attractive as we approach this threshold, leading to a certain over-representation of older people in church congregations.

Our confrontation with death brings out perhaps most clearly some of the basic 'threshold phenomena' which typically appear when we approach a transition-point in our

---

[3] Shakespeare, *Hamlet*, Act III, Scene 1.

experience: our thinking becomes infected with doubt, uncertainty and confusion; our feelings with antipathy, even repugnance, and our will-power may become paralysed by fear and anxiety. There will be more to say later about these basic phenomena: for now, it is enough to note that although they tend to arise automatically, they can partly be overcome—perhaps need to be overcome—by a conscious taking-in-hand of our own reactions and the strengthening of inner capacities which are our only means of keeping hold of ourselves in the face of threshold patterns. This again is a theme to which we will return.

In the West, the understandable preoccupation with questions of the afterlife has tended to overshadow the corresponding set of issues about what lies on the other side of the threshold which we cross *into* life, at birth or perhaps conception. For the people of those extensive cultures in which teachings about reincarnation and karma are fundamental, the image of a 'beforelife' is a natural complement to that of an afterlife. The monotheistic religions, on the other hand, tend to have little to say about the life before birth, apart from the ongoing dispute underlying the abortion debate about when an embryo becomes a person.

There are notable and noble exceptions to this gap. William Wordsworth, in his fine poem *Intimations of Immortality*, states that:

> Not in entire forgetfulness
> And not in utter nakedness
> But trailing clouds of glory do we come
> From God, who is our home.

He tells us that 'Heaven lies about us in our infancy!' and then describes how this spiritual consciousness gradually fades 'into the light of common day'. In other words, something is carried across the threshold into earthly life, just as most religions claim that the consequences of our inner and outer behaviour are carried in some form across the threshold of death. For Wordsworth, the fading of this pre-birth consciousness was a tragic inevitability: his striving, and broadly speaking that of his fellow European Romantic artists, was to develop faculties of imagination as a mature earthly human being, which could allow people to gain insights and experiences beyond those which are accessible to the physical senses and the intellect.

The prospect of approaching and crossing thresholds of consciousness seems to have an ambivalent effect on us. We tend both to long for and to resist the transition-process involved; as in the above example of the child and the mother. Why do we not sleep in the symmetrical centre of the night, for example, from 8p.m. until 4a.m. instead of 11p.m. to 7a.m.? Usually we delay the threshold-crossing in both directions, perhaps because we find it hard to let go of the day, and then also to let go of the night.

On the other hand, we also *seek* threshold-experience, for example in strong, often rather fear-inducing physical sensations such as roller-coaster rides or bungee-jumping; in the second-hand emotion of action films, virtual-reality games or romantic (not quite in the Wordsworthian sense!) novels; or by altering our consciousness through alcohol or other drugs. Through a wide range of methods, most of us flirt with thresholds by seeking thrills of various kinds that take us into other, less conscious modes of experiencing the world. Interestingly, the supernatural, ghosts, vampires, angels and so on, continues in our materialistic culture to provide a constant supply of themes for highly popular entertainments, ranging from the jokey to the sentimental, from the horrific to the sublime.

The outer threshold

The outer threshold is the boundary to the realm beyond what we can experience with our physical senses and our everyday intellect, beyond what can be measured and predicted. To take an everyday example, we can see objects falling towards the centre of the earth, but we cannot see the force of gravity which makes them do so. Newton described and quantified this force, but he did not explain it. How can objects act upon each other from a distance, even through a vacuum? Through what medium do they 'pull' towards each other? Surprisingly enough, physical science has still not come up with a convincing explanation. Again, we may see and feel a surface—a pane of glass, for instance—as being hard, continuous and impenetrable; but physics will describe it as composed of countless particles, with the distance between these being far greater than their actual size, so that most of the apparently continuous surface is composed of 'empty' space. Even light itself turns out in fact not to be visible: this is why the night sky appears black even though it is flooded with starlight and sunlight, which will illuminate physical objects such as satellites or meteors. Because this does not make sense to our normal sense-based consciousness, science has to rely on concepts such as energy, force, attraction, wavelength and so on. *Concepts*, however, are not physical: they are attempts to express realities from beyond the threshold of the sense-world.

When we consider the organic realm, our reliance on non-physical concepts becomes even greater. We can see the *effects* of phenomena such as tropism, instinct, desire and so on, but we cannot directly see, hear or touch any of these realities in themselves. And in relation to the outer aspect of our own lives, we are constantly at the mercy of forces (they used to be called gods) that we cannot predict or control. For example, we can be certain that between two and three thousand people will be killed on British roads in the coming year: but we have absolutely no way of knowing who those people will be. We may be able to identify higher-risk groups, but for individuals, our normal consciousness can give no clues as to what joys or tragedies lie ahead. The statistics do not help us to predict or make sense of a single individual event.

Similarly, less personal questions—Why is the world as it is? What makes a sunset beautiful? What, if anything, is beyond death? What purpose does human life have?—cannot be answered by sense-based consciousness. Whether we turn to images of divinely-guided destiny, or rely on notions such as chance and causality, our questioning minds meet a barrier to the unknown and unknowable, which is sometimes hard to accept, and for most of us, most of the time, impenetrable. Beyond the barrier is a realm we might call 'mystery', which has occupied philosophers and scientists for thousands of years.

The inner threshold

The inner threshold is the boundary to the subconscious—the psychosomatic realm from which instincts, drives, irrational fears and desires, undigested past experiences and traumas, rise into, and impinge on, our everyday awareness and activity. It is the 'cave' into which D.H. Lawrence described Freud as descending, while the world waited with bated breath to see what he would discover:

> What was there in the cave? Alas that we ever looked! Nothing but a huge slimy serpent of sex, and heaps of excrement, and a myriad repulsive little horrors spawned between sex and excrement.
>
> Is it true? Does the great unknown of sleep contain nothing else? No lovely spirits in the anterior regions of our being? None! Imagine the unspeakable horror of the *repressions* Freud brought home to us. Gagged, bound, maniacal repressions, sexual complexes, faecal inhibitions, dream-monsters. We tried to repudiate them. But no, they were there, demonstrable. These were the horrid things that ate our souls and caused our helpless neuroses.[4]

This graphic if rather pessimistic account of the subconscious may have been somewhat revised since Freud's initial findings, and subsequent explorers from C.G. Jung onward may have claimed other discoveries, including treasures, at deeper levels of the cave. Nevertheless this realm continues to be regarded with wariness in most cultures, as a source of primitive, unpredictable and often unsocial impulses. It is the seat of what some religions would call original sin, whose influence needs to be countered by prescribed codes of behaviour and sanctions for non-compliance.

Religious or not, most of us would have to admit that self-examination reveals significant traces of subconscious influence in the way we conduct ourselves. What truly motivates us, guides our choices, strivings and patterns of

---

[4] D.H. Lawrence, 'Psychoanalysis vs. morality' in *Psychoanalysis and the Unconscious*, Dover, 2006.

behaviour in life? How many of our decisions are really determined by fully conscious considerations, as distinct from feelings, urges, wishes of mixed or unknown origin? The night world of the subconscious lives and works in us continually.

The relational threshold

Lessons from the fireplace: relationship creates warmth
In lighting and tending a log fire, we discover the importance of structure, complexity and distance in sustaining combustion. If the logs are put too close together, they will stifle each other and stop burning. Equally, if they are too far apart, they will be unable to mirror each other's heat, and will sooner or later cool down and go out. A lively blaze requires enough different elements, the right distance from each other, to allow the circulation of air and the exchange of warmth. When this is the case, the fire can fulfil its task of warming the room. Similarly, when people find the right degree of closeness and separateness, they can gain warmth from each other and also serve the wider society most effectively. How often do we actually allow this principle to inform the way we develop our relationships, formal and informal, private and professional?

The third and central proposition of this book is that:
A third type of threshold exists between human beings. The other person is an unknown world; and meeting this—especially in profound, intense ways—confronts us with actual and potential experiences that challenge and deepen our sense of self, and demand that we learn and change.

What happens in us when we meet another person? If we watch ourselves carefully, we can observe two opposite tendencies which arise as it were automatically, whenever we are confronted with another human being. These can perhaps be noticed in their 'purest' state when we are introduced to a stranger, in a context relatively free from preconceived or remembered impressions: however, they are always present at some level in any interaction, whatever the status of the existing relationship.

One of these tendencies we will call *sympathy*, using this term not in the everyday sense of feeling sorry for someone, but in the broader sense of being drawn towards them, being attracted, interested, intrigued, involved, engaged, affected. This type of sympathy is instinctive, perhaps intuitive, not the result of conscious consideration or choice. It is something we discover in ourselves, and may then decide what to do about it.

The other, opposite tendency will here be called *antipathy*, again not in the common sense of dislike, but more generally the impulse to withdraw, keep to oneself, resist being influenced, maintain boundaries, close off from the other. Sympathy and antipathy with these meanings are complementary impulses in us. Neither is better or worse than the other: we need them both. Without sympathy we could not form relationships at all: without antipathy we could not sustain our own sense of identity. For our present purposes, the important point is that these forces simply *appear* at the relational threshold, and then challenge our conscious awareness to manage them effectively.

They do not always appear in a balanced, healthy or helpful way. When sympathy has the upper hand, we may lose ourselves in the other person, allowing them to over-influence or manipulate us. Entertainers, orators, salespeople and others exploit this tendency, for positive or negative purposes. At its best, allowing ourselves to be carried on the force of sympathy expands our sense of being and potential, makes us feel connected with a wider community—a theatre audience, a family, a political or religious movement. On an individual level, it makes it possible for us to experience something of the soul-world of the other person, to meet and appreciate them. At its worst, it robs us of our powers of discrimination, leading to blind faith in charismatic leaders, to gullibility, fanaticism, mass hysteria. Think of the rise of Nazism, for example; or Stalin's astonishing command of so many people's affections, despite his brutality; or more recently the influence of 'fundamentalist' religious or cult leaders. The urge to identification is very powerful, especially in a time of strong individualization with its accompanying syndrome of loneliness.

When the force of antipathy is strongest in us, temporarily or chronically, we become stuck in ourselves, unable to enter a real relationship. The tendency to criticize and reject anything we have not personally created, builds walls between us and others. Healthy scepticism becomes endemic cynicism; we assume that all politicians are liars, all salespeople are con-artists, all men are sexual exploiters, all women emotional manipulators, all managers egotistic power-seekers, and so on. Strangely enough, our experiences then often tend to confirm these prejudgements!

Antipathy is the force on which we rely, to distinguish on a psychological level between the 'I' and the 'not-I', just as the immune system in the body distinguishes between what belongs and what does not belong to our physical organism, and rejects foreign invasions. When this system is damaged or deficient, as in the case of AIDS sufferers, we become vulnerable to potentially fatal infections. Similarly, when our antipathy-system breaks down, we can become possessed by patterns of thinking, feeling and behaviour which are not chosen or controlled by our individual consciousness. This image is perhaps one way of understanding such initially incomprehensible phenomena as cult followings or suicide bombing missions.

We rely on sympathy to bridge the gulf between ourselves and others: when we lose the ability to use this faculty, the result is some form of mild or more extreme autism. Recent studies[5] have suggested that alarmingly high numbers of adult males exhibit significant symptoms of Asperger's syndrome, in their inability or reluctance to communicate or engage with others. Over 200,000 people in the UK are diagnosed with this syndrome: males outnumber females by more than nine to one.

Milder forms of this tendency include computer game / internet addiction, excessive TV watching, and the drying-up of communication between couples. A medical parallel might be the cancerous process, which is one of a self-enclosed vicious circle, in which diseased cells become alienated from their wider context, redirecting the organism's resources to propagating themselves instead of interacting healthily within the whole body. Another relevant comparison is with the increase in cardio-vascular illnesses in Western societies over recent decades. This type of disease is less prevalent in societies, and in individuals, which have retained stronger elements of community and family iden-

---

[5] Robert D. Putnam, *Bowling Alone: The Collapse and Revival of American Community*, Simon & Schuster, 2001.

tification. James Lynch describes this phenomenon in his book *The Broken Heart*.[6]

Parental warmth affects future health

In the early 1950s, multiple-choice scores reflecting feelings of warmth and closeness with parents were obtained from a sample of healthy undergraduate men. Thirty-five years later, detailed medical and psychological histories were obtained. Of the participants, 91% who did not perceive themselves to have had a warm relationship with their mothers (assessed during college) had diagnosed diseases in midlife (including coronary artery disease, hypertension, duodenal ulcer, and alcoholism), as compared to 45% of participants who perceived themselves to have had a warm relationship with their mothers. A similar association between perceived warmth and closeness and future illness was obtained for fathers. Since parents are usually the most meaningful source of social support in early life, the perception of parental love and caring may have important effects on biological and psychological health and illness throughout life.

Journal of Behavioral Medicine 1997, Vol. 20, 1

In adolescence, the dynamic between sympathetic and anti-pathetic responses to the world and to other people shows itself quite dramatically. On the one hand, young people strive to establish their individual identity, often strongly rejecting the values, norms and conditioning of their upbringing. Parent-child relationships may become strained to the point of alienation. Friendly children turn into sullen, silent or hyper-critical teenagers. Rebellion and self-assertion are expressed through clothing, hair and body decoration,

---

[6] James Lynch, *The Broken Heart: The Medical Consequences of Loneliness*, Basic Books, 1979.

challenging behaviour, and so on. At the same time, strong or extreme sympathies also show up—the peer group becomes all-important, with its accompanying uniforms and conventions; there may be obsessive devotion to sporting or musical celebrities; early sexual and emotional relationships produce exhilarating and devastating effects. We are constantly close to the relational threshold during this period of our lives, and the extent to which we succeed in learning how to recognize and manage its forces, developing what Goleman and others have called 'emotional intelligence',[7] will have a far-reaching effect on our future.

Sympathy and antipathy are the two poles of relational energy. This bipolar nature of our soul reactions parallels many scientific accounts of what lies beyond the sense-perceptible aspects of the material world, across the outer threshold. In what follows, we will explore more specific manifestations of these and their accompanying threshold phenomena, and attempt to characterize how they underlie many contemporary social issues—from sexuality, marriage and divorce, to racism, crime and violence.

---

[7] Daniel Goleman, *Emotional Intelligence: Why it can matter more than IQ*, Bloomsbury, 1996.

3. Threshold Phenomena

Karl Koenig, in his book *The Human Soul*,[8] complains that much contemporary psychology does not study its own subject. ('Psyche' is simply Greek for soul, so psychology is 'soul-science'.) Focusing only on outwardly observable behaviour diverts us from researching the inner realities of the soul directly. Yet we all have souls, and our experience of soul-phenomena is arguably more direct, accessible and reliable than that which is mediated and potentially filtered or distorted by our outward-oriented senses. In any case, all science relies on at least one soul-process: thinking. If thinking is not real and valid, no reliable statements about the world are possible. If it *is* real and valid, we can apply it with at least equal validity to our observations of the inner world as we do to the world of matter.

The threshold of thinking

Inner observation shows us a complex, dynamic eco-system of forces, processes and phenomena, which, you will no doubt be relieved to hear, it is not intended to elaborate here. Nevertheless certain main features can be identified, at least in the conscious part of the soul ('above' the Inner Threshold). The first has already been mentioned: the realm of thoughts and thinking. Human thinking has the remarkable capacity— as far as we know, unique in the universe—of being able to perceive itself directly. We can follow our own thoughts, and

---

[8] Karl Koenig, *The Human Soul*, Floris Books, 2006.

identify the inner tools and processes used for thinking: ideas, concepts, categories, mental pictures, language and other symbols, memories, logic, imagination, and so on. Thinking is a *lawful* activity, and the same laws apply whoever is doing the thinking: this is why scientific and mathematical consensus is possible, if not always achieved. Once we have thought through, for example, the reality that the internal angles of a triangle always add up to 180 degrees, it is literally not possible, unless one is mentally ill, to think otherwise. Thinking represents our most objective, impersonal way of relating to the world, and of communicating with others. It is most effective when applied to reflecting on past experience, on observations made or information received.

When our thinking approaches a threshold—for example, when new evidence undermines our existing concepts, or someone tries to convince us to adopt a new set of ideas—our first reaction is usually one of doubt, scepticism, possibly denial. Historically, such reactions have greeted most new discoveries, inventions and scientific theories. Habitual patterns of thought are difficult and uncomfortable to change. In management circles, practically every year sees the emergence and promotion of some new approach which requires managers to 'repent' (literally, change one's thinking, from the French *repenser*) and embrace a paradigm shift and a new set of ideas and techniques proposed by would-be John the Baptists (the original consultant!). Not surprisingly, most of them resist such invasions of their existing mind-set, at least until their bosses and/or their business performance make change obligatory. They draw back from the threshold of new thinking with all its unknown and unknowable consequences, both inner and outer.

For all its apparent objectivity, thinking is underpinned by a phenomenon which lies deeper in the psyche and is less immediately accessible than the intellect. We might call it intuition, or perhaps, a sense of rightness, or, a feeling for truth. This is the sense which allows us to confirm the validity of a particular thought in accordance with the lawfulness mentioned earlier. The laws of thinking are not ones which have been thought up and written down like social laws, though people have of course attempted to formulate them. Rather, they exist as realities in a realm across the threshold which Georg Kuehlewind calls the 'super-conscious', the realm of meaning.[9]

Computers have no feeling for truth: they will follow the logic of their programming wherever it leads. The dependence of human thinking on an intuitive feeling for truth saves our human intellect from becoming inhuman and mechanical. It also confirms that the human psyche is a unity, whose interweaving elements can be distinguished but not divided.

The threshold of feeling

The second of these elements is the subjective aspect of the soul, the realm of feeling and emotion, through which we experience joy and sorrow, love (in the everyday sense of the word) and hate, anger and compassion, and so on. Rather than the sense of truth, feeling endows us with the sense for beauty, in the widest possible meaning of this word. Beauty cannot be captured by logic; it is in the soul of the beholder.

Although feeling often appears undervalued in our

---

[9] Georg Kuehlewind, *From Normal to Healthy: Paths to the Liberation of Consciousness*, Lindisfarne Books, 1988.

intellect-based culture, it is almost always the ultimate basis of our decisions: we choose our dwellings, our jobs, our purchases and, above all, our relationships, on the basis of what we believe will bring us satisfaction and happiness. Feelings even underlie apparently rational economic decisions, because profit is an increase in satisfaction: when we try to maximize our wealth, in other words, it is because of the positive feelings which its possession and use can bring. Equally, feelings underpin most of our moral and political choices: human rights, justice, public policy, are all ultimately questions of what *feels* fair or appropriate. The values by which we live are centred in our feelings, and from there become consciously formulated in ideas on the one hand, and expressed through our behaviour on the other. These two opposite directions can of course lead to inconsistencies, in which the ideas we claim to believe in are not reflected in what we do. This is called hypocrisy; a contradiction between word and deed which results from a mismatch between thought and will in the soul.

In a relational context, a central issue which we will explore in more depth later is that of *trust*. Trust is not an objective phenomenon. I cannot convince you to trust me by means of logic: if you don't trust me, you don't trust me, and no amount of argument is likely to change that. To know whether or to what extent we trust someone, we have to consult our feelings. This reality points to another—that *feelings can be organs of perception*. However, they will only be reliable organs if they are consciously developed and deployed: otherwise, they may convey only prejudice and projection. Paradoxically, feelings are the most personal aspect of our inner life, yet they can only serve us best when we succeed in refining and raising them to a level at which they transcend the personal: for example, in appreciating a work of art, in devoting ourselves to a deeply held ideal, or in empathizing with another human being. Again, more on this later.

Feelings are less conscious than thoughts. It is not always clear to us what is happening in our feelings—some of us are more in touch with this realm than others. Sometimes we can be influenced by a feeling, an underlying anger or frustration, for example, for some time before it rises into consciousness. We cannot always explain or understand our feelings; they sometimes seem to have a life of their own, and we 'discover' that we have lost our temper, or become depressed, or fallen in love. One way of describing this would be to say that if we are awake in our thoughts, we are dreaming in our feelings. Becoming conscious of these dreams means lifting them into the realm of thought. The statement 'I am angry' is in fact a thought, the inner observation of a feeling, translated into a concept.

Sympathy and antipathy, the primary phenomena of the relational threshold, are of course feelings. More precisely, we could perhaps say that they arise in the feeling realm of the psyche: but they lead us in opposite directions. In order to think clearly, to make objective observations about the world (including ourselves and other people) we need a degree of antipathy, of withdrawal, standing back, separating ourselves from the subject of our thoughts. Antipathy enables thinking to free itself from other aspects of our inner life; it is a cooling, distancing type of energy which, if it becomes predominant, can lead to a soulless intellectualism. Sympathy on the other hand leads towards the third and least conscious realm of the soul—the will.

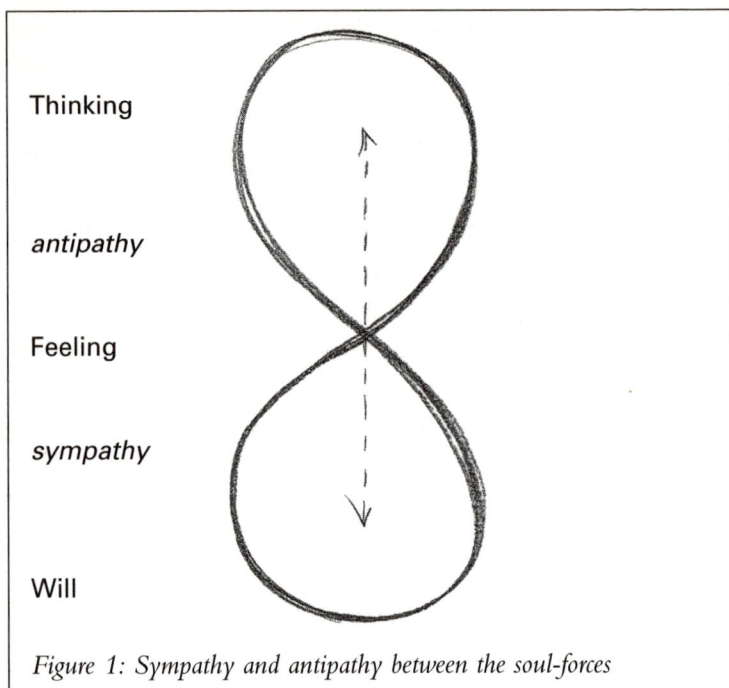

Thinking

antipathy

Feeling

sympathy

Will

Figure 1: Sympathy and antipathy between the soul-forces

The threshold of will

Where do our real motives and impulses to action originate? What makes us get up in the morning; work to meet our responsibilities even when we do not feel like making the effort; commit to goals, ideals and relationships? Thoughts and feelings play a part in all of these, of course, but ultimately the energy to translate them into action comes from a soul-region which is not directly accessible to our consciousness. We may *understand* the need to stop smoking, or *feel* deep concern for the environment or human rights, and yet fail to translate the thought or wish into concrete action. Quite simply, we lack the will.

Motivating ourselves from inaction to action always involves meeting and crossing a certain threshold, often minor and routine, but sometimes crucial and life-changing. We can all look back at moments in our lives where the exercise, or not, of our will created real turning points: whether we spoke out or held back, stayed in or left a situation or a relationship, said Yes or No to a proposal, persevered in an endeavour or gave up. We may be able to rationalize our decision afterwards, but in the moment itself, the will is decisive—either it engages or it does not. At this threshold, we confront the issue of goodness rather than truth (thinking) or beauty (feeling). Awakening the sleeping realm of the will means attuning our motivation to what is good—for ourselves, for others, for the world. To the extent that we are able to do this, we can claim to be guided by self-chosen values rather than only unconscious instincts and drives.

Whereas thinking is always past-oriented—even when we think about the future, we use images and concepts which we have already acquired—and feelings come and go in the present, the will is what creates future realities. Not a huge amount of poetic licence is required, to say that *the future lies asleep in our will-forces*. The most basic, everyday form of clairvoyance consists of listening to others in such a way that we intuitively 'read their fortune' by perceiving the seeds of the future which live unseen in the soil of the soul, below the threshold of the will.

Synergy of the three thresholds

Where have we come to so far in this threshold-survey? There have been several 'threes', and there will be more, so a summary may be helpful at this point. The main observations and characterizations so far have been:

1. A threshold is the boundary between one state of consciousness and another, often 'higher' or 'lower' state.
2. The outer threshold is where our awareness reaches the boundary of that kind of knowledge which is mediated by the physical senses and the intellect. This is traditionally the boundary between physical science on the one hand, and the metaphysical, that is, religion or spirituality, on the other.
3. The inner threshold is where our self-awareness meets the subconscious realm of instincts, drives, phobias and collective archetypes.
4. Between these two, lies the realm of the psyche and its basic processes of thinking, feeling, and will. Each of these can lead us to thresholds where our existing patterns and habits are challenged and potentially changed.
5. The dynamic feeling-polarity of sympathy and antipathy is activated by encounter, especially with another person: this creates the phenomena of the third, social or relational, threshold.

Shakespeare's play *Macbeth* gives the supernatural credibility through its combination of acute psychological observation and its depiction of a man whose conscious scruples are overwhelmed by his own ambition and the influence of his 'fiend-like' wife. The interaction of the three thresholds compounds the unfolding tragedy.

Emily Bronte's *Wuthering Heights* portrays the devastating power of the subconscious in the violent rages of Heathcliff, which is mirrored by the forces of nature on the windswept moors, and the compelling, transforming, obsessive reality of an intense relationship: the whole novel is transfused with dimensions beyond our ordinary experience.

The most powerful and moving works of art have always been *in-formed* by threshold experience, often addressing two or all three of the thresholds. Great music can carry us out of ourselves into an imaginative state for which the physical sound is only a vehicle. From Sophocles to Pinter, drama explores the ways in which subconscious forces shape our destiny. The infinite range of agony and ecstasy in relation-ships is played out in countless love-stories, poems, dance, and theatre performances. Painting and sculpture through the ages have depicted all of the above.

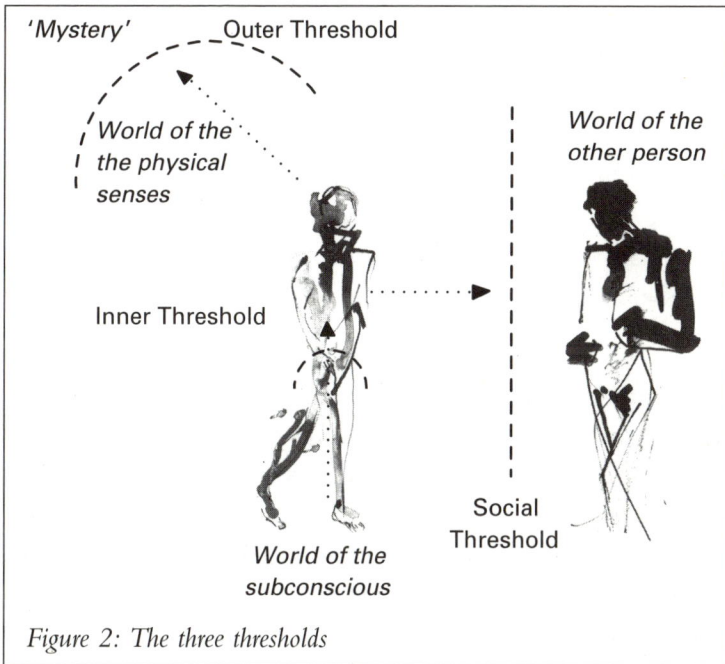

'Mystery'   Outer Threshold

World of the the physical senses

World of the other person

Inner Threshold

World of the subconscious

Social Threshold

Figure 2: The three thresholds

4. The Archetype of the Social Threshold

Meeting my child's new class teacher for the first time; I want and need to be open to him, to like him, to trust him. Yet the voices inside say:

- he's pretending something—he's not really as wise and experienced as he's trying to appear;
- that bow tie is a ridiculous affectation, and he seems to be an incompetent shaver;
- he's not as warm and kind as my little girl deserves, he won't really appreciate how special she is;
- he'll be too harsh with her—or too indulgent, and steal her affection from me . . .

At the same time, I'm impressed and a little overawed. I allow him to patronize me mildly, and laugh at his jokes although I don't really find them funny. I play the model school parent and leave the meeting with mixed feelings, about the teacher and about myself.

If we carefully observe and examine the processes which take place in our thoughts, feelings, and will when we meet another person, we can identify some basic or typical phenomena. On a conscious, thinking level, we may experience a mixture of interest and scepticism, with various factors, including subjective ones, determining the balance between these two. Is what the person communicates true, accurate, meaningful? Or do we doubt their knowledge and authenticity? In our feelings, we will almost always sense the dynamic between sympathy and antipathy—being drawn towards, and/or repelled by the other person—which has been described above. In the will, we may find ourselves motivated to engage with them and develop the relationship in some way, and/or inhibited by subtle or strong anxieties which undermine any impulse to act.

Rudolf Steiner characterized this type of experience in a rather startling and radical way: 'When two people come face to face, each of them works on the other in such a way as to put the other person to sleep; and the other is constantly striving to keep himself awake.'[10] Borrowing a phrase from Goethe, he describes this dynamic as 'the archetypal phenomenon of social life'. Elsewhere, he refers to the tendency that we have so far called sympathy as the 'social forces' in the human being, and the antipathy pole as 'antisocial forces'. Again, these should not be interpreted as morally positive or negative: we need both.

The social, sympathy-forces activated by encountering another person draw our attention outward, away from our own concerns and soul-processes: if this were to continue unchecked, we would lose ourselves—lose our own consciousness as we do when we fall asleep. To prevent this, the antisocial antipathy-forces pull us back into the realm of our own thoughts and self-awareness, where we are awake. Steiner's picture is that this is an automatic process; elsewhere he describes it as a 'vibration' of the soul—perhaps comparable to an alternating electric current—which signals to us the presence of another individuality. This oscillation between

---

[10] Rudolf Steiner, 12 December 1918, *Social and Anti-Social Forces in the Human Being*, Mercury Press, 1982 (GA 191).

sympathy and antipathy, sleeping and waking, other and self, takes place at what we have called the social or relational threshold.

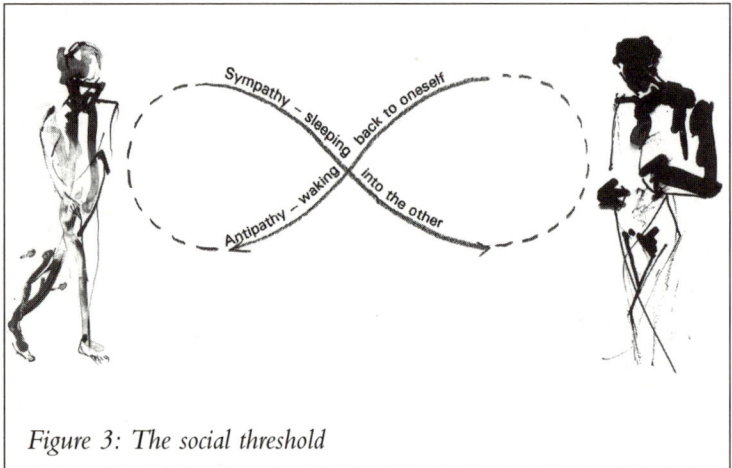

Figure 3: The social threshold

Two questions will probably arise in you at this point: firstly, is this description true, verifiable? and secondly, of what use is it?

Verifying the Phenomena

At university, an ongoing debate with a friend who was studying philosophy turned on the question 'What do we mean by "mean"?' It turned into a running joke—'What do we mean by "mean by mean"?' and so on. Twenty-five years later I asked him whether he had ever found an answer. Now an eminent public servant, he replied 'I think it is a matter of what you *do*.'

Thinking alone cannot create meaning: the will must also be engaged, so that ideas can become ideals . . .

It should already be clear that what is described in this book is not based on empirical or statistical research, but primarily on direct observation of oneself and others. As such, its main content can in principle be confirmed directly by personal experience. This type of confirmation may not arise immediately, but will often require reflection, inner experimentation, and an openness to new and perhaps unfamiliar perceptions. Ultimately, our ability to grasp social and spiritual reality and make meaning out of our experiences depends on our own activity. This is a book for practitioners, not theorists. It is our inner and outer practice which generates the evidence for the realities I am trying to describe.

One everyday experience which can be heightened by self-observation into a source of evidence for the social archetype, is the demanding activity of *listening* with full attention to another person. Listening not only to the content of what is being said, but also trying to discern the underlying feelings and intentions of the speaker, takes a level of focus and concentration which most of us rarely muster. Typically, we quickly find our attention fragmented between the other person's reality and our own: thoughts, judgements and emotions arise in us which may be reactions to what we hear, but have their origin in our own concerns and experience. When this happens, we are listening to ourselves, not to the other person. True listening involves quietening our own internal voices to create an open space inwardly, in which we can be fully focused on someone else. Yet the more intensely we try to practise this, the more overwhelming becomes the urge to withdraw and reclaim the inner space for ourselves. If we succeed in staying with the other person through the force of sympathy, we may experience the threshold of 'falling asleep' into their reality, and/or the transition in the other direction where we are thrown back into ourselves as if waking from an intense dream.

A more extreme example, not quite so available for everyday experimentation, is that of falling in love, in which the sympathy-forces become so predominant that we blissfully lose ourselves in the relationship. We feel enchanted, transported to another realm of being. We may experience a feeling of oneness with the beloved. These are all threshold phenomena—the crossing of a boundary to a different mode of consciousness. Those around us may experience us as indeed asleep to the risks, realities or morality of our situation. Falling out of love again is often a rude awakening, after which it is hard to imagine how we could ever have felt and behaved the way we did. The lovers in the wood in Shakespeare's *A Midsummer Night's Dream* experience exactly this pro-cess—repeatedly!

An even more disturbing experiment can be to try to imagine the consciousness of a torturer—to picture oneself deliberately inflicting extreme pain, and to create an image of the state of mind which would need to prevail, to allow such actions. Clearly, sympathy would have to be all but com-pletely extinguished: the torturer must be entirely gripped by their own aims and rationale. The victim has to be dehumanized, felt as an object unconnected by any common experience to the perpetrator. Here, the threshold has become almost impermeable. Reflection on this inner imaginative exercise can lead to the recognition that we all inflict unnecessary pain on others, negligently if not intentionally, at certain times. This can occur because we 'bounce back' from the relational threshold and remain caught in our own experience.

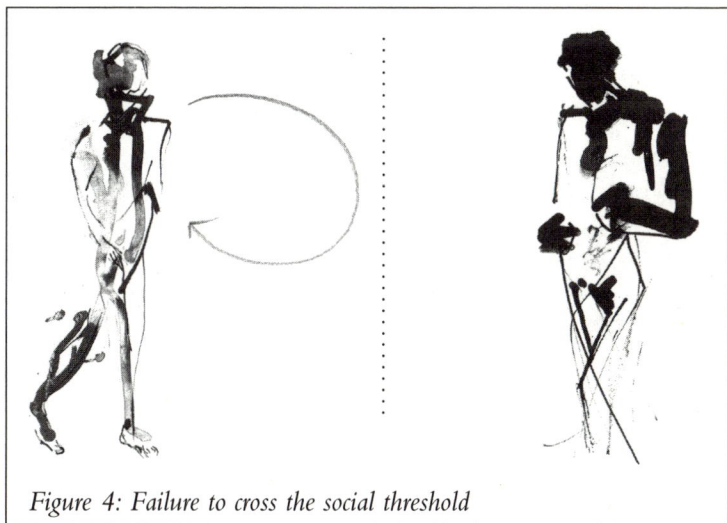

Figure 4: Failure to cross the social threshold

Threshold phenomena in the three soul-forces

The forces of sympathy and antipathy work into the ways we think, feel and act, producing different patterns in different relationships and different situations. Some of the more extreme effects are described in the table below; but we can all recognize milder forms of these tendencies, for example, when we find someone attractive and are inclined to be taken in (slightly put to sleep!) by their ideas; or when we feel threatened by a dominating boss or partner and would like to set stronger boundaries, but somehow fail to muster the will-power to confront them.

	When sympathy is strongest the result may be:	When antipathy is strongest the result may be:
In our thinking	Blind faith, naivety	Doubt, disbelief, scepticism, cynicism
In our feeling	Infatuation, euphoria	Hate, dislike, alienation
In our will	Recklessness, obsession	Fear, paralysis

If we pay attention in ways like this to the phenomena of sympathy and antipathy in our own souls, we can in time achieve a kind of independent verification, or indeed modification, of what has been described so far. The further crucial question then becomes: how can we use these insights in our own relational practice?

Working with the phenomena

One of my former colleagues is addicted to giving advice: whatever your problem, she will have an answer ready for you almost before you have finished describing the question. She is quite intuitive and often her suggestions are genuinely helpful; but she is so enthusiastic about selling them that sooner or later people switch off and withdraw, or avoid consulting her altogether. Those who remain open to her often find themselves, sooner or later, in a rather dependent relationship.

Thresholds need careful handling: if they are crossed negligently there can be unfortunate consequences. For example, if the social/relational threshold is crossed too far and without permission, people feel psychically *invaded*. The other person's intervention, however well-intentioned, is felt as intrusive, even oppressive. In these cases, the sympathy-forces are being pulled too strongly. The pressure to agree, to accept, to 'buy' the other person's ideas, experience or motives produces the opposite reaction: our own antipathy-forces intensify in response, and to avoid being put to sleep, we half-automatically reject their influence, even if intellectually we know they are right. Protecting our sense of self-determination requires waking back into our own soul-space, where we can experience a relative independence of thought, judgement and decision. However, if our antipathy-forces are weak, and/or the external influence highly effective, we may allow ourselves to become conditioned by the other, losing ourselves in their depiction of the world and their definition of morality. Hypnotism is an extreme example of the collapse of antipathy: religious fanaticism is another, though in this case the antipathy may be turned strongly against other world-views, whilst one's own cult is accepted uncritically. In such an unbalanced inner state, human beings can exhibit frighteningly extreme behaviour.

The opposite of invasion is *deprivation*, in which a weakness of the sympathy-forces or an exaggeration of antipathy prevents a healthy traffic across the interpersonal threshold. The boundary becomes almost impermeable: unable to reach each other, people are trapped in themselves, longing for true engagement from and with others, but powerless to achieve it. Countless children have suffered from this syndrome in the emotionally disengaged parent, leaving them inexplicably bereft and damaged far into their adult lives. Ironically, this pattern seems most prevalent among those who are far from deprived on a material level.

In an early scene of Willy Russell's play (and film) *Shirley Valentine*, the heroine talks to her kitchen wall. Although she has a husband and a son and some friends, something essential is missing. She does not feel *met* or recognized for who she really is or could be. Her search for true encounter and human warmth takes her to the physical warmth of Greece and a brief affair, before her husband arrives and finds his wife a changed woman, who requires change from him also if their relationship is to resume.

This image of the two opposite problems, invasion and deprivation, can become a helpful basic orientation in managing our relationships. It is useful to start by observing the phenomena in oneself: in what situations, and in which relationships, do I feel invaded, over-demanded, too much drawn out of my own centre? In which do I feel deprived, ignored, unheard, unacknowledged? How do I react to each of these? What (different) behaviour from the other person would help me to feel more open, and more truly met? Then of course comes the crucial question: when and how may I be causing others to feel invaded or deprived? Could this explain some of the reactions I am experiencing from them? What could I do differently? We can make this into a little reflective exercise for ourselves, by listing some key or problematic relationships and identifying the invasion/deprivation patterns in both directions. This could lead to some attempts to change our own behaviour, or even more constructively, to some open dialogues with the people concerned.

My teenage son, not untypically, has become more and more resistant to guidance from his parents. To preserve at least some communication, we back off in all but the most crucial issues. When he mentions various options for university courses, I try to listen with interest and make encouraging but non-directive responses. I know that if I express a view he will quickly reject it. Finally, in some frustration, he asks: 'Dad, don't you have *any* opinions about what I should study?'

'Of course I do,' I reply, 'would you really like to hear them?'

Moving from the individual to the group level of relationships, these phenomena appear just as strongly. Invasion and deprivation are the negative aspects of crossing, or failing to cross, the social threshold. The effects of social boundaries—organizational, cultural or racial—enhance and potentially aggravate these issues. As noted in the first chapter of this book, the boundaries we create to give ourselves a feeling of belonging also create barriers to relationships with 'outsiders'. We tend to feel sympathy, in other words, for those in our own group, even if we experience personal tensions with them, and antipathy for those whose allegiance is elsewhere. This is an obvious, universal and often tragic phenomenon. What is less often acknowledged, perhaps just because of its universality—is the immediacy with which such feelings arise. People who work in the field of management development can observe the astonishing speed with which a group of seminar participants, arbitrarily divided into two for the purpose of, for example, a negotiation exercise, quickly develop competitive and adversarial attitudes to their colleagues in the other team. 'Them and us' phenomena are all too readily created by organizational boundaries: this is a reality to which designers of corporate or institutional structures need to pay careful attention. Patterns often emerge, such as Operations feeling invaded by Marketing and deprived by Maintenance, while Human Resources over-sympathetically tries to compensate, and everyone feels invaded by Finance... More on this in Part III.

On the macro-social level, these patterns can become even more severe. Invasion can become literal, physical, and deprivation existential. Israelis feel threatened, because they are: Palestinians feel both invaded *and* deprived, because they are... The threshold phenomena of suspicion, hatred and fear can become self-perpetuating; the perceived enemy becomes demonized as deceitful, wicked and threatening. Even in largely safe and peaceful societies, forces from across the inner and outer thresholds often seem to *require* that such an enemy be always present and continually in the public awareness. This can then justify authoritarian legislation, aggressive foreign policy and ever-increasing military expenditure.

A less extreme but highly instructive example of threshold phenomena in boundary issues is the dynamic of the development and expansion of the European Union. Can we and should we, in the context of a global economy, extend our sense of identity beyond the nation-state to a wider social and political reality? Where should the new boundaries be positioned, geographically and juridically? Some populations start to feel invaded by what is seen as a super-state: others feel deprived by not (yet) being admitted to the Community. Perhaps it is not an exaggeration to suggest that questions like these can only be adequately understood and addressed on the basis of a real appreciation of the phenomena of the social threshold, and the development of the insights and skills to which such appreciation can lead.

Returning to the personal and interpersonal dimension, the next chapter explores how we can try to manage our soul-forces more consciously in developing constructive relationships, and in diagnosing and trying to heal destructive ones.

5. Relationships at the Threshold

Having explored the phenomena of sympathy and antipathy, 'sleeping' and 'waking', invasion and deprivation in the context of human encounter, we can enquire more closely into the dynamics of what happens at the different levels of the soul in a relationship. Again I will be referring to common experiences which can be followed and confirmed by anyone who is open to unprejudiced inner observation. Although the following description will suggest a certain sequence of responses, our thinking, feeling, and will are of course all activated simultaneously by meeting another person. However, the sequential account does indicate the way in which the different levels of reaction affect and lead on to each other.

In every relationship, three levels of reality are continuously interacting: the perceptions which people form about each other, the attitudes which they develop towards each other; and the behaviour of each person in relation to the other. *Perceptions* arise on the thinking level—they are relatively conscious, but they may be accurate or distorted, full or partial, based on observation and/or interpretation. People's mutual perceptions—how they see each other—are a basic factor in any relationship. *Attitudes* can be positive or negative, open or closed, trusting or suspicious. They tend to be formed on the basis of perceptions, but build up over time into an inner reality on the subjective, feeling level which can be hard to change: try changing one of your own, to see how intransigent attitudes can be! *Behaviour* is the outwardly visible level in a relationship: it tends to be influenced by a person's perceptions and attitudes, as well as their own intentions and decisions.

The illustration below describes how these levels affect each other: *my behaviour* is seen and interpreted into *your perceptions*; these affect *your attitude* towards me, which in turn influences *your behaviour*. This leads to perceptions and attitudes in me that influence my behaviour—and so the cycle continues, leading to constructive or destructive patterns which often become self-reinforcing.

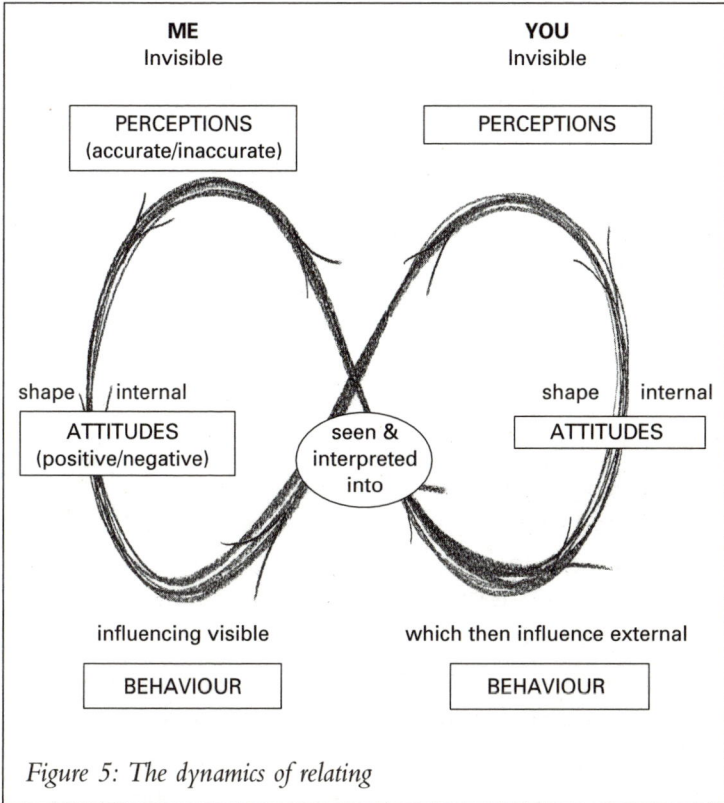

Figure 5: The dynamics of relating

Where can I start, if I want to change or improve the quality of a relationship? In fact, the only element in the six-step cycle that I can directly control is my own behaviour. To change someone else's behaviour, we usually have to start by changing our own, thus creating different perceptions that lead to changed attitudes, which may induce the other person to behave differently. A helpful exercise can therefore be to work backwards initially, through the cycle, and ask oneself the following questions:

1. How does s/he currently **behave** towards me?
2. What **attitudes** may underlie this behaviour?
3. What **perceptions about me** may s/he hold, which give rise to these attitudes?
4. What aspects of **my behaviour** could be creating or reinforcing these perceptions?
5. What **new perceptions and attitudes** do I want to create in him/her, and what can I do more, or less, or differently, to achieve this?
6. If I succeed in changing his/her perceptions and (in the longer term) attitudes, what **new behaviours** could I expect—or negotiate and agree—with him/her?
7. How and when should I take the first steps?
8. How might I recognize progress in improving the relationship?

Trust and distrust—benign and vicious cycles

We can learn a lot about the dynamic described above, by observing what builds and what destroys *trust*. Firstly though, we need to distinguish between different types of, or bases for, trust. If I do not trust my three-year-old with power tools (though he would love to get his hands on them and protests loudly when he cannot), this is not a moral judgement but one about *capacities*. Equally, when I asked a tradesman not to drive his van so fast on the drive leading to our house, because there were often children playing there, and he told me that he had never hit a child yet and did not intend to, my reply: 'It's not your *intentions* I'm worried about, Chris...' was about the limits of his, or anyone's, ability to cope with the unforeseen, not about his good will. If I do not quite trust my fourteen-year-old to come home at night at an agreed (actually imposed, usually) time, this is partly a question of moral responsibility and partly again a matter of her capacity to resist whatever temptations might delay her return. I may trust a stranger to keep an eye on my belongings while I go to the buffet car on the train, but I ask this because I do not quite trust every one of my other fellow travellers not to steal them.

Trust and distrust are realities on the feeling level which arise out of our perceptions of the other person. I decide to trust the stranger on the train because they look honest, which in practice often means they look like broadly the same kind of person as me! In longer-term relationships, I will make an initial assessment and perhaps later various re-assessments as to whether I trust their honesty and their integrity: do their words match their thoughts and their actions? However, even if they pass these tests, there may be something missing in my image of them which inhibits full trust. This missing element could be called *authenticity*. Even someone whose words are accurate and deeds consistent, will not gain my full confidence unless I can somehow experience the richer, deeper reality of their personality. When I 'sleep into' them and 're-awaken' to myself, what impressions do I bring back? Are there elements I can connect with and relate to—a sense of humour perhaps, or a degree of modest self-awareness, a certain idealism or human warmth? Trust, which appears as a feeling, is most fully confirmed and consolidated by being able to perceive and endorse the other person's feelings. Only then do we see them as a full human being, worthy of our trust.

This is of course a central aspect of trust-building. To gain the genuine trust of our customers, partners, staff members or electorate, we need to be seen as more than just effective professionals. Appropriate self-disclosure is important, and this rests on genuine self-knowledge: otherwise it is mere posturing or manipulation. Trusting relationships are characterized by the open sharing of feelings, from the trivial to the deep and intimate. Correspondingly, asking and telling about feelings, without invading privacy, and without pretence, is one of the best ways to deepen and humanize a relationship. Combined with honesty and integrity, it is a powerful trust –building activity. It opens a window through which one is willing to be seen, and makes the social threshold permeable.

Managing the relationship process

We have said that the only part of the six-step cycle of encounter that we can directly control is our own behaviour, and that this must therefore be the starting point for any initiative to develop or improve a relationship. Given the difficulty of addressing attitudes directly, such initiatives will usually need to begin by working on the levels of perception and/or behaviour. Perceptions can be shared, clarified and sometimes adjusted, through mutual feedback. This is a vital but risky process in any significant relationship. It needs to be approached with both caution and courage: caution because feedback given or heard in an unbalanced way can be highly destructive; and courage because one needs to be ready to receive as well as to give, and to cope with possible reactions to anything perceived as negative or critical, even if it is not meant as such.

Unwanted feedback is usually experienced as invasive, so the principle of consent is important. Invitation is even better. Balance, the giving of examples, and questioning rather than labelling are helpful guidelines, and are set out in many books on assertiveness and similar approaches. For our purposes, it is enough to note that in working on perceptions we need to respect the threshold whilst making it more transparent. Seeing each other clearly and accurately is an essential asset for any long-term relationship. It is also one of the most important elements which can support self-development, because it helps each party to see themselves more fully and clearly. Ultimately there can be a glimpse of the potentially infinite in human relationships here: when I know that you know that I know that you know me, and so on, there is no necessary end to the depths of encounter which are open to us. More on this in Part II.

The other level at which relationship development can be initiated is the level of behaviour. Behaviour can be negotiated. Again, much has been written about this elsewhere, so we will not go into the various principles and techniques involved. In the context of threshold exploration, however, it is significant that nearly all the important decisions which affect our lives today, whether on the personal, professional or wider social or global level, are the result of some kind of negotiation carried out somewhere between human beings, i.e. across the Third Threshold, whether we have been personally involved or not. Again, this must be seen as part of the ongoing process of individuation: we need to become less and less dependent on convention, habit or authority in managing our relationships, and more and more competent and confident in making constructive agreements in our families, workplaces and communities.

Empathy

> I don't believe in evil, but I do believe in ignorance. The root of evil I think is ignorance ... of right and wrong, and also I think ignorance of other people's feelings. I suppose you could call it lack of empathy. If you could feel for others as you would feel for yourself, then there is very little room for evil, because evil is mostly what you do to others.
>
> Aung San Suu Kyi
> (Leader of the National League for Democracy, currently (2010) under house arrest in Myanmar, or Burma)

The term *empathy* was first used in the early twentieth century in the context of the emerging discipline of psychology. It was popularized especially by the psychotherapist Carl Rogers in the 1950s and is defined in the Oxford English Dictionary as *'the power of projecting one's personality into, and so fully understanding, the object of contemplation'*. By contrast, 'sympathy' has been used in English since the sixteenth century, and applied to a much wider sphere of reference, including non-human phenomena such as chemical elements. The common modern usage is defined as *'the quality or state of being affected by the condition of another with a feeling similar or corresponding to that of the other'*. The difference between the definitions is striking, and points to an essential differentiation for the purposes of this book. Sympathy arises through 'being affected'—in other words, it is something that happens to us rather than an activity we undertake. Empathy, on the other hand, involves 'power', not passivity, and 'projecting' is something we consciously do in order to understand what we are actively contemplating.

The other important distinction is that sympathy draws us into a kind of identification with the other person—'affected . . . with a feeling similar . . .'. If we sympathize with a grieving person, we become sorrowful ourselves. There is nothing wrong with this, but it is not necessarily the most helpful response to the person in question (any more than trying to cheer them up would necessarily be!). But to take another example, if we are gripped by sympathy for a person who is filled with anger or self-righteousness or hatred, we may 'sleep into' a state for which we cannot freely take responsibility.

In a dialogue on these questions with an old friend, he described the force of love as 'a confusion of identity', a merging of oneself with the beloved. This is indeed the primeval infant experience of love and being loved, and is sometimes repeated later in life, at least temporarily, through the experience of being in love, but the image of the individuation process, described in Chapter 1, suggests that the experience of separation is a necessary process on the path to a more mature type of love which includes freedom. Most mothers have no choice but to love their babies: this is beautiful and inspiring, but it is not yet moral as such. Love-in-freedom requires both antipathy and sympathy, in the rather technical way these terms are defined above. We can love our families and friends out of sympathy, but loving one's enemies requires the conscious cultivation of an objective empathy.

Military commanders in the twentieth century were dismayed to learn that up to 75% of conscripted soldiers were deliberately firing wide of the enemy, to avoid killing. Special training strategies were needed, to desensitize them into becoming effective combatants—starting with simple measures like using human figures for target practice. This desensitization continues today in thousands of children's toys, films, and computer games, in which killing is presented as necessary, noble, exciting and satisfying, and even as trivial or amusing. Hatred of the enemy is not necessary or even reliable as a weapon of war. What is essential, however, is the elimination of empathy.

How is empathy developed? (I write here not as an expert or master of empathy, but as a student practitioner with many failed, and some more successful attempts so far.) One precondition seems to be a familiarity with sympathy and antipathy, to be able to recognize them as forces in oneself when they arise, and to be able to resist, at least to some extent, being overtaken by them without giving one's inner consent. This can and needs to be practised. Secondly, it is necessary to be able to harness these forces more consciously, and bring them under a degree of conscious control. For example, if I want to understand a person I instinctively dislike, I will need to restrain my automatic antipathy and summon a degree of self-chosen sympathy in order to cross the threshold into their inner world. Paradoxically, this can actually prove easier than the opposite challenge of bringing

distance and objectivity into a relationship where one natu-
rally feels sympathetic: for example, when a friend is in distress. Thirdly, I need to be able temporarily to suspend my
own feelings and reactions, quieten my own soul-voices and
clear a space in which the other person's reality, not a projection of my own, can become visible. These are all
important preparations for conscious threshold-crossing.

The empathic process then seems to proceed in something
like the following steps—set out rather schematically here for
the purposes of explanation, but in reality a flowing, organic
and infinitely varied experience:

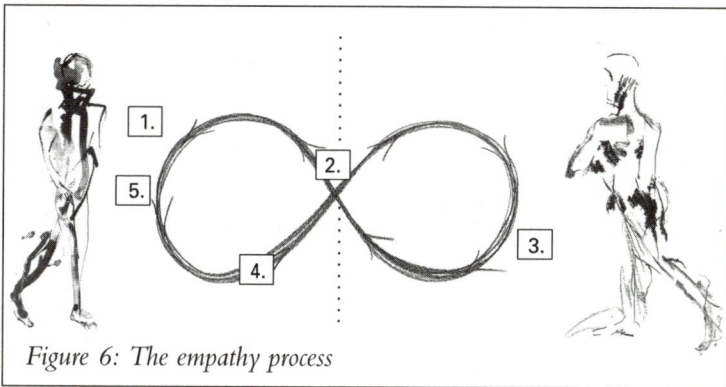

Figure 6: The empathy process

1. Inwardly turning to the other person: creating a mood of
   inner calm and openness, free of prejudgement: putting
   aside our own personal agenda;
2. Crossing the threshold on the force of sympathy, by
   careful attention to the words, voice, expression and
   gesture of the other person: entering into their inner
   reality;
3. Experiencing the soul-world of the other: living imaginatively in their thoughts, feelings and will-impulses;

4. Returning to oneself!—via the force of antipathy, which restores our self-possession, and enables:
5. Reading the after-image, which has been imprinted in our own consciousness by the journey which has been made.

Only when all these five steps are undertaken in some form, can we genuinely perceive the other person's reality. It sounds a tall order, and it is, but everyone can do this to some extent. We probably do so daily. Also, this empathic capacity can always be further developed, whatever our inborn level of individual talent for it, by conscious cultivation and practice. The process may be deliberate and meditative, or it can be instantaneous and rapidly-repeating, or rhythmic and flowing throughout the course of a longer conversation or consultation.

Of course, there are many obstacles and pitfalls at each of the steps. Quietening our own psyche, and keeping it quiet, can be extremely problematic. Holding back judgement can feel like holding our breath. Summoning sympathy in some situations can be a real challenge, and staying for any length of soul-time (which may only be a fraction of a second in clock-time) in an alien reality can be disturbing, even frightening. Our only safety-belt in this undertaking is a secure sense of self, the confidence that our own unique individuality is a reality which can never be merged, lost or isolated unless we choose to allow this.

The benefits of practising empathy are of course double-sided. For ourselves, the primary gain is of insight: whether we are trying to understand the problems of a client, friend or family member, or to get inside the mind and motivation of a political opponent or even a criminal, empathy can be applied effectively to provide insights which intellectual analysis could never reach. For the other person, being listened to empathically can be deeply supportive, even healing in itself. It is an essential basis for all coaching, counselling or therapeutic work, for all helping conversations. Especially when combined with sensitive feedback, it can help the other person hear themselves more clearly, and thus open up opportunities for conscious change and personal development.

Empathy cannot be mandatory . . .

In the British public sector, 'care providers' deliver 'care packages' according to fixed criteria applied by 'care assessors'. In 2007 Blair's government issued an instruction to NHS nurses to smile. A cabinet spokesman explained, 'One of the things that came out of the focus group discussions was that they didn't feel nurses gave the impression that they cared enough. They felt, for example, that they should smile more.' This was followed by the announcement that nurses' smiley-ness ('empathetic care') would be measured and the scores published on an online 'compassion index'.

'If some jumped up bean-counter comes near me with a "compassion index"', a nurse blogged on the *Guardian* website, 'he'll get it administered rectally.'[11]

---

but empathy is universal . . .

Sitting on the tube train reading, with my briefcase on my lap, I suddenly realize we've arrived at my stop and jump up to get off, grabbing the case but failing to fasten the lid first. It seems to explode, scattering the contents all over the carriage—papers, diary, pens, gadgets, spectacles. . . . Instantly, everyone

---

[11] Adam Phillips and Barbara Taylor, *On Kindness*, Penguin, 2009.

dives in to help—a school kid, a black guy, an Asian woman, an old man—hearing my yelp of dismay and seeing the urgency. They all grab things and throw them back into the case, someone hands me a pen just in time, as I bundle it all up and stagger out of the doors as they close. No time even to say thank you. I'm on the platform gasping as the train pulls out, clutching my stuff and grinning both at my own slapstick behaviour and at the unexpected friendship of strangers. Moments before we had all been sitting in isolation, avoiding eye contact, in separate mental worlds; then a trivial emergency created instant, temporary community, in helping one individual in trouble. I like that image: amid all the divisions and threats of the world, six months after the bombings on the underground, it seemed like a microcosm of humanity showing spontaneous solidarity.

Meeting the shadow

Meeting another person in a more than superficial way always involves exploration into the unknown. Across the Third Threshold are mysteries, realms of experience which are profoundly foreign as well as others which are very familiar. Working in the thoughts, feelings, and intentions of a human being will be deeper forces from across the other two thresholds: the higher values and ideals which inspire our moral and spiritual strivings; and also the lower impulses, often denied or unacknowledged, which limit and threaten our social and individual development. These negative forces—greed, cruelty, vanity and many others, traditionally known as sinfulness—are common to us all, but take on a unique configuration in each person. This configuration is referred to in many esoteric traditions as the Double or shadow being of an individual: the opposite, positive forces may be called the 'angelic' dimension.

Encountering the Double can be a shocking experience. The veils of convention and inhibition are torn away, and the person appears in their least worthy aspects. This may happen in a fit of rage, in which spiteful, vengeful feelings are expressed ('I wish he was dead!') or simply an unguarded moment in which a sneering, arrogant phrase slips out. The more sympathy one has previously experienced towards the person, the more devastating can be the sudden revelation of their lower nature—when an idealized husband or wife is unfaithful, for instance, or a revered religious teacher is proved to be hypocritical.

Because the revelation of the Double can be so powerful, it is easy to be knocked off balance by it. We recoil into antipathy, perhaps even feeling we want nothing further to do with the person. This is an understandable but not always a helpful reaction. Certainly the new perceptions may lead us to make new choices about the relationship; but the tendency to imagine that we are now seeing 'what they are really like' is dangerous. The Double is a part of everyone: it is not the whole of anyone. It is certainly real, and sometimes appears overwhelmingly so: but it is not the whole reality, nor necessarily any more real than the positive values and developmental efforts which are also present, though not always visible, in everyone. Seeing it as definitive of any individual is no more realistic than denying its existence.

In every close, long-term relationship, the Double of each person will sooner or later become visible to the other. This may happen in a mild or a more severe form, but it cannot be avoided altogether. What can perhaps be avoided is the extreme distress or disappointment which the revelation can cause. The key here is acceptance: the Double represents the developmental challenge which each of us faces, to transform ourselves gradually into what we would freely choose to be. Facing and accepting one's own Double is the starting point for the capacity to meet and work positively with the other person's. True meeting involves risk, requires courage and creates the opportunity for transformation, for on the journey across the Third Threshold we discover the Beauty of the other person, but also the Beast.

'Beauty and the Beast'[12]—a parable of encounter and transformation across the relational threshold

Here, a summary of the story is interspersed with a commentary on the Third Threshold imagery and insights which it contains.

A rich merchant lived in a city with his three daughters, two of whom are mean-spirited and selfish, however the youngest is named Belle (Beautiful) for being lovely and pure of heart. The merchant eventually loses all of his wealth in a tempest at sea, and he and his daughters must therefore live in a small farmhouse and work for their living. After some years of this, the merchant hears that one of the trade ships sent by himself has arrived in port, having escaped the destruction of its compatriots; therefore he returns to the city to discover whether the ship contains anything of monetary value. Before leaving, he asks his daughters whether they desire that he bring them any gift upon his return. His two elder daughters ask for jewellery and fine dresses, thinking that his wealth has returned; Belle is satisfied with the promise of a rose, as none grow in their part of the country. The merchant finds that his ship's cargo has been seized to pay his debts, leaving him without money with which to buy his daughters their presents.

During his return, he becomes lost in a forest. Seeking shelter, he

---

[12] *Beauty and the Beast (La Belle et la Bête)* is a traditional fairy tale. The first published version of the fairy tale was a rendition by Mme Gabrielle-Suzanne Barbot de Villeneuve, published in *La Jeune Américaine, et Les Contes Marins* in 1740. The best-known written version was an abridgement of Mme Villeneuve's work published in 1756 by Mme Jeanne-Marie Leprince de Beaumont, in *Magasin des enfants, ou dialogues entre une sage gouvernante et plusieurs de ses élèves*; an English translation appeared in 1757.

enters a castle. Inside he finds tables laden with food and drink, which have apparently been left for him by the castle's owner. The merchant accepts this gift and is about to leave when he sees a rose garden and recalls that Belle had desired a rose. Upon picking the most lovely rose he finds, the merchant is confronted by a hideous 'Beast', which tells him that for taking his (the Beast's) most precious possession after accepting his hospitality, the merchant must stay his prisoner forever.

After his generosity to the distressed merchant, why is the Beast so outraged at the plucking of the rose? Is it simply a ruse to get the guest's daughter to come to the castle? The narrative does not explain, but we have all experienced someone getting upset about what seems to us a triviality. Often, deeper reflection can lead us to see something which, in our self-preoccupation, we had overlooked, something that was in fact highly significant for the other person. The merchant, in entering the realm of the Beast, has taken *what was not offered*—he has abused the welcome he received, and unwittingly committed a kind of invasion of his host's inner space (garden).

The merchant begs to be set free, arguing that he had only picked the rose as a gift for his youngest daughter. The Beast agrees to let him go only if the merchant will send his daughter to live in the castle in his place. The merchant is upset, but accepts this condition. He tries, upon arriving home, to hide the secret from Belle; but she pries it from him and willingly goes to the Beast's castle.

The merchant's visit to the Beast is out of necessity, driven by his own need. In contrast, Beauty freely chooses to make the journey into this alien realm. She shows courage, integrity and trust in doing so—the qualities required in preparation for crossing the relational threshold . . .

The Beast receives her graciously and treats her as his guest. He gives her lavish clothing and food and carries on lengthy conversations with her. Each night, the Beast asks Belle to marry him, only to be refused each time. After each refusal, Belle dreams of a handsome prince who pleads with her to answer why she keeps refusing him, and she replies that she cannot marry the Beast because she loves him only as a friend.

Beauty's openness and goodwill allow the Beast to become visible—not in rage, as with her father, but in his dual nature—the features of the Beast, the words and tone of the Prince. Her acceptance of this, her ability to see past his appearance, is the first step towards his redemption. Marriage, however, is the most profound demonstration of acceptance by one person of another. In asking this, the Beast is asking: 'Do you really love me? Do you *really* accept me?' Beauty is not yet ready for this ultimate step in their relationship.

Belle does not make the connection between the handsome prince and the Beast and becomes convinced that the Beast is holding the prince captive somewhere in the castle. She searches for him and discovers multiple enchanted rooms, including one filled with birds singing, another with paints, brushes and easels ready for use, and a third with spinning wheels, looms and thread for weaving.

This could be an image of the third step in the process of empathy, described above as experiencing the soul-world— the thoughts (birds), feelings (colours) and will-impulses (craft work)—of the other.

For several months Belle lives a life of luxury at the Beast's palace, being waited on hand and foot by invisible servants, having no end of riches to amuse her and an endless supply of exquisite finery to wear. Yet eventually, she becomes homesick and begs the Beast to allow her to go to see her family. He allows it, if she will return exactly a week later. Belle agrees to this and sets off for home with an enchanted mirror and ring. The mirror allows her to see what is going on back at the castle, and the ring allows her to return to the castle in an instant when turned three times around her finger. Her older sisters are surprised to find her well-fed and dressed in finery. They grow jealous of her happy life at the castle, and, hearing that she must return to the Beast on a certain day, beg her to stay another day, even putting onion in their eyes to make it appear as though they are weeping. It is their wish that the Beast will grow angry with Belle for breaking her promise and will eat her alive. Belle's heart is moved by her sisters' show of love, and she agrees to stay.

The sleeping/awakening dynamic of threshold-crossing is here explicitly portrayed. In this fourth phase of empathy, Beauty leaves the realm of the Beast and returns to her own home. Only from this place of antipathetic self-possession can she make clear choices.

Belle begins to feel guilty about breaking her promise to the Beast and uses the mirror to see him back at the castle. She is horrified to discover that the Beast is lying half-dead of heartbreak near the rose bushes her father had stolen from and she immediately uses the ring to return to the Beast.

In her reading of the 'after-image', Beauty sees the effects of her abandonment. The profile of the Beast is now completely reversed: he is no longer the predator or abductor but is now himself a victim, captured by his dependency on her. Having been invaded by the father, he is now deprived by the daughter, with near-fatal results.

Quickly she puts on the ring and awakens back at the castle. She runs through the grounds calling for him, and finds him lying, close to *death, under a tree as in her dream. Her tears of love revive him and he tells her he can now die happy having seen her again. 'No!' she says, 'you shall not die. I **will** marry you.' At this, the Beast recovers and is transformed into the handsome prince, his real self...*

The story culminates with the transformative effect of full acceptance. The Prince is the Beast, and the Beast is the

Walter Crane, illustration for 'Beauty and the Beast'. London: George Routledge and Sons, 1874.

Prince. It is important that Beauty's acceptance of marriage comes *before* the transformation, indeed before the possibility of transformation is even apparent. Her motive is to save him (not the best motive for a real marriage!) not to get herself a prince. It is compassion that leads to acceptance of the Beast in the other person, and acceptance that leads to the revelation of the true, higher self.

II

THE THRESHOLD OF INTIMACY

6. Families at the Threshold

Parenting, step-parenting and the question of freedom

A conversation with my stepdaughter:
—You don't love me as much as John [her little half-brother] cause you're his real Daddy and not mine.
—I know you feel that, sweetie; and sometimes I feel you don't love me as much as your 'real' Dad... But I'm real too... It's true that I don't love you in exactly the same way that I love John; but that doesn't mean I love you any less—just differently...

The love of parents for their biological children is—with very few tragic exceptions—universal and visceral. For most, it is automatic, instinctive, inbuilt. Evolutionary scientists and selfish-gene theorists find this easy to explain: but how does it affect the Third Threshold phenomena we have been exploring? Where does genetic programming end and freedom begin, if indeed there is space for freedom amid the intense emotions of family relationships?

The step-parenting experience is enlightening here. In many ways, my little girl was quite right—however loving and kind, a step-parent can never be the full equivalent of a natural parent. The automatic, physiological connection and the sympathy-forces it releases are simply not present in the same way. In my own child, I see the reflection of my own genetic material: although this is not always a pleasant experience, it is always an intimate one. It binds together, for good or ill, my relation to my child and my relation to myself. If I am uncomfortable with certain physical or personality traits in myself, I may find them difficult in my child. I may even try to compensate for my own self-perceived short-comings in the way I behave as a parent. I have made an irrevocable investment of a part of myself in my own off-spring, and I will inevitably see them and relate to them through the distorting lens of this natural connection.

For many mothers, the threshold phenomena of relating to their child begin already during pregnancy, when women often experience periods of 'meditative brooding', dreamy moods in which their consciousness becomes less focused on the practical and the intellectual, and floats into an imagi-native or intuitive sense of identification with the new human being who is developing inside them. Though not universal, this experience does seem to be archetypal. It is filled with the warmth, often the joy, of unconditional sympathy. Once the baby is born, most mothers go through a powerful bonding process and feel a strong sense of identi-fication with their child, which is reinforced by the intimate connection built through the rhythms of feeding, changing, sleeping, and rocking. In my experience, fathers can experience a reflection of this intimacy if they are closely involved with the care of the small child; and later, the 'automatic' parental connection can become more evenly balanced between mothers and fathers.

With a step-child or foster-child (and perhaps an adopted child, though I cannot speak from experience there), the starting situation at least is significantly different. The auto-matic, genetically-based sympathy is not there. This means that the achievement of intimacy, the building of a parental relationship, takes more effort. It may include the over-coming of some weaker or stronger antipathies, sometimes on both sides. It also needs continuous attention and rein-forcement. Although parents and their natural children can become estranged, a biological relationship will usually more or less guarantee a continuing close connection. A step-child, however, can never be taken for granted, at least if one wants the relationship to be more than the circumstantial connec-tion which is mediated by the common link with the natural parent.

The positive aspect of this lack of automatic sympathy, however, is the extra element of freedom which it brings and requires. I have to *decide* to love my step-child, whereas I have almost no choice with my own offspring. The commitment to parenting, full or partial, of a child not biologically one's own, is comparable perhaps to the commitment one makes to a spouse or partner, but without the in-love-ness that precedes it. One may not even initially *like* the child in question (though it certainly helps if one does). The full spectrum of the Third Threshold will play itself out; from warm connectedness in moments of harmony, to experiences of estrangement and even rejection when things go wrong.

It can be hard to have confidence in our own real feelings in such a dynamic. If I sometimes feel like rejecting and closing off from the child, can it really be true that I love them? Yes. It can, if we are able to accept that love is not a feeling but a decision. When I *feel* like rejecting the child, but do not; when I sustain my commitment without the support of a natural connection; when I make the effort to treat them like my own child even though they are not—these are expres-sions, arguably, of a love which is different from, but not less than, the love I give my 'own' children. That is what I tried, rather clumsily, to convey to my little girl in the exchange at the start of this chapter. I'm not sure how much she understood, at age ten, though she did somehow seem to take it in.

Can love be free?

Love as decision not feeling: that needs exploring further! It means that in terms of the three soul-forces (described in Part I, Chapter 3), love, or what we might call love-in-freedom, is ultimately a matter of *will*. Clearly it is not primarily a matter of thinking, although clarity of thought could be said to be a precondition for any free choice. But is it not deeply rooted in our feelings? Certainly, but if I have no choice about loving someone—my own child, or someone I have fallen in love with—then that love is by definition not free. If loving involves effort, commitment, sacrifice, it must be based on an act, or rather, repeated acts, of will. This is why the step-parenting experience is so revealing. It demonstrates the difference between conscious and unconscious, between free and automatic, crossing of the Third Threshold.

When we see our own children in distress or pain, we feel their suffering as if it were our own. This is something that happens to us, not something we need to choose. Where the blood connection is absent, a more conscious development of empathy is called for, which can certainly, over time, become established in our souls. Not only step-parents, but carers, teachers, clinicians and most workers in the caring professions will experience the need to develop this. It is not fashionable today, and might even be considered slightly suspect, to speak of loving one's pupils, patients or clients: but this is actually what empathy in such contexts means—the journey across the Third Threshold, not to gain something for oneself but in the service of the other human being.

This picture leads to further questions in the context of family relationships: how possible is it, and how is it possible, to act out of freedom in relation to one's own blood-relatives? Thousands of books, hundreds of research programmes, and millions of hours of therapy have of course been devoted to this question. What can be added, from the perspective of the threshold-phenomena we are exploring here?

The subconscious and the self-conscious in family relationships

When family relationships become intense or problematic, we often seem to be adrift in a stormy sea of feelings. Waves of emotion arise and subside: strong tides of anger, sorrow or longing draw us along or pull us into the depths. Reliable landmarks are often absent: notions of what we 'should' or would like to feel are rarely helpful. Conflicting currents drag us in different directions, sometimes into whirlpools of self-defeating spirals. Keeping our head above water can take all of our available energy.

Self-observation is the first step towards self-rescue from this turbulent sea: to extend the analogy, we must somehow not only be the survivor amid the waves, but also the helicopter pilot who looks down from above—and ultimately even the rescuer who descends to winch us to safety.

Many approaches to healing the soul, especially in addressing the effects of difficult family relationships, call upon memory and the feelings associated with earlier experiences. For

example, the inhibiting or distorting influence of a domin-
eering parent can last well into adult life, if not addressed by
therapy or conscious self-development. Such an influence
cannot simply be rejected or discarded, because it has become
embedded in the subconscious realm, from where it works
across the Inner Threshold into the dark, sleeping area of the
soul where our sympathies draw us, for better or worse, into
new relationships. These relationships can then become
infected with unhealthy patterns—dependency, revenge, or
oppression—which work against our conscious intentions,
but originate in our own past experiences working uncon-
sciously in our soul.

Self-observation, initially through memory, can be a path
to illuminating and ultimately addressing such barriers to
freedom in our relationships. Whether guided by a therapist
or undertaken on our own inner initiative, the practice of
investigative self-observation can bring light into realms that
may have been dark for decades. What is revealed by this
light can be difficult and painful to contemplate; for instance,
the realization that a beloved parent was actually subtly
abusive, or that repressed resentment against a sibling whom
we saw as more successful or more loved has caused recurrent
bouts of depression. The consequences of such insights may
need time and often support from others, professional or
otherwise, to work through; but they are a precondition for
transformation and healing.

Self-observation of our own soul-processes, past or
present, of course presupposes that there is a part of our
human nature which is capable of standing 'outside' or
'above' our immediate experience and contemplating not
only our own actions but also our own thoughts, feelings and
motives. As described in Part I, Chapter 3, such contem-

plation becomes more problematic as we shift from the awakeness of our thinking, through the dreaming realm of feelings, to the sleeping forces of will. Nevertheless, we can at least partially perceive our own inner activity. It would be outside the scope of this book to discuss in depth the important question of what element in the human being is capable of self-perception—a question curiously overlooked by many psychological and philosophical systems. For our purposes, we will refer to this element as the *individuality* or *ego*—though emphatically not the same as what Freudian or popular psychology mean by this term.

If self-observation is, at least potentially, capable of bringing light into the dark realm of sympathy, it is also able consciously to bring warmth into the otherwise cold field of antipathy, in which we stand alone and separate from others. In relation to our past experiences, it is possible to cultivate what we might call a 'loving antipathy'. This means that when, having lived into and explored our earlier experiences

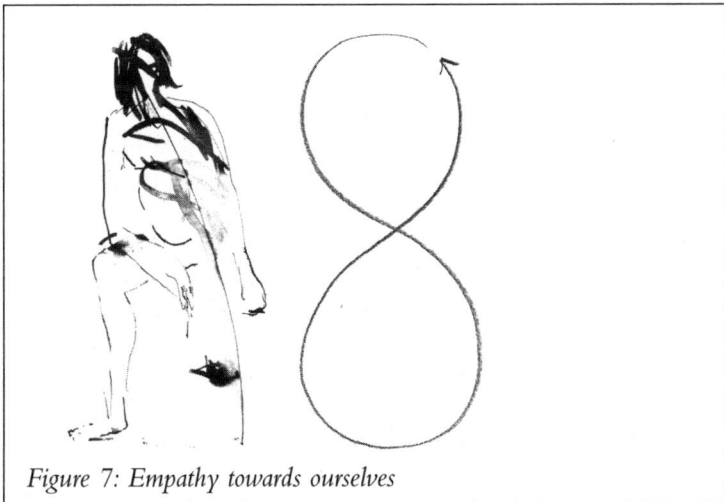

Figure 7: Empathy towards ourselves

and feelings, we stand back and 'read the after-image' in empathy with our former selves, we try to bring to this process of reflection a quality of compassion; both towards ourselves and to the family members or others who were part of the earlier relationship dynamic. Only the individuality, the 'I' itself, not the soul alone, is capable of this act of freedom.

The rhythmic movement between exploratory 'sleeping-into' the configuration of one's sympathies, and reflection on these in 'loving antipathy', can lead to healing. In a sense, it is the archetype of the psychotherapeutic process, whether this takes place in formal sessions guided by a professional, or on a personal, individual basis as self-healing. Its outcome can be a growing force in the soul, which we might call forgiveness. This force can then sink down into the subconscious and gradually dissolve the negative patterns embedded there.

A middle-aged woman, facing the latest of several crises in her relationships with male partners, consulted a therapist in the hope of being helped with a difficult decision. With his help, she explored the feelings she had for her current partner and for someone new she had recently met and fallen in love with. Torn between her sense of loyalty and appreciation for the man she was with, and the deep longings and hopes that the new relationship prompted in her, she had been agonizing for months about the choice she needed to make.

Through the process of remembering, exploring, and reflecting on her emotional biography, an unexpected out-come emerged. Part of her unfulfilled hopes and needs in relating to men was connected with childhood experiences of a distant and often disapproving father. Until she was able to face and transform this reality, which had taken root in her unconscious sympathy-life, she could not make truly free decisions about future relationships.

Gradually, with the help of her therapist, she was able to penetrate some of her past and present emotions with the insight revealed by inner exploration, and to work through her initial reactions of anger and resentment towards the father she had hitherto idolized. A turning point in her healing process came when she made a conscious, freely-chosen decision to extend the compassion she felt for herself as a little girl, to the father who had made her feel inadequate—and had no doubt experienced his own suffering, which inhibited the expression of his love for his daughter. Before he died, she was able to tell him that she forgave him. It didn't matter so much whether he fully understood: a new sense of freedom had awoken in her, and could support her future choices.

The threshold between siblings

Tennis—and many similar sports—provides a graphic illustration of the threshold archetype. The court with its equal space for each player, divided by the physical threshold of the net, can be seen as an image of the two soul-realms in a relationship. The spherical—head-shaped!—ball, with its infinite variability of direction, pace and spin, has characteristics in common with the endless flexibility and adaptability of human consciousness. The rackets or bats, extensions of the human limb, express the force of will-power; and the flow of play across the central threshold mirrors the rhythm of sympathy and antipathy.

A good tennis shot requires first the observation and anticipation of one's opponent's strategy, intentions and actions. Except when 'serving' (wonderful term!), we cannot choose the position and timing of the ball when we meet it. We need to 'live into' the opponent's game. As in dancing and negotiation, we will not succeed by simply insisting on our own position, but by being willing to be moved by, as well as to move, our opposite number; constantly to let go our own self-determination in order to meet what comes across the threshold, often in unexpected form, from the other person.

Then, having made the 'sacrifice' required for meeting, we move into the antipathy-phase. In our own realm, in the split second we have in which to decide on our own stroke, comes the moment of free decision, lob, drive, or drop-shot, in which we assert ourselves and give our opponent something to respond to. We might call this back-and-forth process the conversational archetype. In sport, it is of course given a competitive framework, arguably a sublimation of combat without the bloodshed, but the process itself, in what it requires of and stimulates in the players, is a brotherly/sisterly, developmental, social dynamic.

In healthy family contexts—if one can refer to such, avoiding the unhelpful notion of 'normal'—brothers and sisters squabble, fight, make up, compete, co-operate, create fantasy games and secrets, develop an acute sense of fairness and unfairness, learn to appreciate differences, build a shared language and culture, and generally prepare themselves and each other for integration into the wider society at school and beyond. In doing all this they are of course making use of a primary practice-field for managing the threshold between themselves and others.

Every sibling relationship is of course unique, and each will have its own particular dynamic in the flows of sympathy and antipathy. These can range from 'inseparable' intimacy through fractious rivalry to alienation and indifference. As a general picture, however, we can say that the safety of the family context, and the 'automatic' connection created by the blood relationship, seems to allow a wider swing in the oscillation between identification and separation than feels safe with other peers. 'I hate you, you pig!' screams the nine-year-old at her little sister, secure in the awareness that no one will believe her—least of all the girl, who completely ignores the outburst and calmly persists in the behaviour her sister is finding so irritating. Ten minutes later they are happily giggling and playing together with increasing wildness, until a parental admonishment to one of them provokes the reaction: 'Not fair! She was doing it too. . .'.

The boy who will mercilessly tease and boss around his younger brother at home, will fiercely defend him in the school playground. The girl who 'hates boys' with pre-pubescent antipathy, will nevertheless look up to and admire, with a mixture of awe and horror, the macho posturing of her older brother. The Third Threshold between siblings is highly permeable, and the rhythm between association and self-assertion is often quite uninhibited. Like tennis players both hitting full-blooded ground strokes from the baseline to the back of their opponent's court, brothers and sisters stretch and stimulate and entertain each other, whilst developing their own threshold-management capabilities.

'Sibling rivalry' is a cliché that represents a reality. In our relations with brothers and sisters, the whole potential and problem of social interaction is rehearsed. As the story of Cain and Abel powerfully illustrates, the results can be profoundly tragic, with devastating long-term consequences for the family of mankind. If all men are fundamentally brothers, all wars are fratricidal. In terms of positive social ideals, *liberty* and *equality*, and the apparent (though ultimately illusory) trade-off between them, are familiar reference points: but what of *fraternity*? It seems to be the least realized, perhaps because least understood, of the three great ideals of the French Revolution. In relation to the theme of this book, fraternity/sorority means serving each other, across the Threshold, with stimulus, challenge, respect, closeness, difference, surprise, recognition, support, and mutual learning. Rivalry may be inevitable between siblings: our threshold-task, from childhood on, is to help each other transform it into a force that nurtures, rather than stultifies, personal and social development.

7. Couples at the Threshold

> I saw in his hand a long spear of gold, and at the iron's point there seemed to be a little fire. He appeared to me to be thrusting it at times into my heart, and to pierce my very entrails; when he drew it out, he seemed to draw them out also, and to leave me all on fire with a great love of God. The pain was so great, that it made me moan; and yet so surpassing was the sweetness of this excessive pain, that I could not wish to be rid of it...
>
> St Teresa of Avila

Three levels of love

Religion, sex and love are all fields of experience that carry us across thresholds into altered states of consciousness. Perhaps for this reason, they are often connected, both personally and culturally. There are of course three different thresholds involved. Religious, mystical experience, direct or reported, gives us glimpses of forces and beings beyond the Outer Threshold of the material world. Sexual impulses release forces from below the Inner Threshold between conscious and subconscious. The experience of love for another person carries us irresistibly across the Third Threshold. When these distinct—but not always divisible—threshold-crossings are combined, the results are profound and life-changing.

Following the writing and dissemination of the *Book of the Zohar* in the fourteenth and fifteenth centuries, Jewish mysticism took on a strongly erotic element, and the Song of Songs came to be regarded as an example of sacred *erotica*. In Zoharic Kabbalah, God is represented by a system of ten *sephirot*, or spheres, each symbolizing a different aspect of God, who is perceived as both male and female. The *Shechina*, or indwelling of God on earth, was identified with the sephira *Malchut*, which is female in essence, and symbolizes both the Jewish people and the female sexual organs. Malchut was, in turn, identified with the woman in the Song of Songs. Her beloved was identified with the sephira *Yesod*, which represents God's foundation and the phallus or male essence. The text thus became a description of an act of divine eroticism, symbolizing—depending on the interpreter—the creation of the world, the passage of the Sabbath, the covenant with Israel, or the coming of the Messianic age.

In the traditions of many religions, including Hindu, Judaic, Islamic, and Christian, erotic and mystical imagery are often combined to express the intensity of relationship between the divine and the human.

> The erotic carvings of medieval Indian temples, such as those of Khajuraho in central, and Konarak in eastern, India, have always puzzled people of other religions. If there is one clear and unambiguous message in the sensuality of these sculpted representations, it is that the human soul is pre-eminently amorous, and nothing if not amorous ... the sexual act in Hindu religious tradition does not lie outside but within the holiness of life ...
>
> Sudhir Kakar

Are we to regard this simply as a kind of analogy, or are there real, substantial connections between these realms which can often seem so far apart? This is a rather modern question: until the last century, few people would have questioned the reality of a spiritual dimension in human relationships; perhaps calling this God's will, destiny, or karma. More recently, a kind of territorial struggle developed between competing world-views, with Christianity, for example, continuing to represent marriage as a human reflection of Christ's love for the Church, and sexuality as a gift of God for the purpose of procreation within marriage; whilst Freudian psychology, in contrast, suggested that, for instance, the mystical narratives of St Teresa with their imagery of being pierced by the angel's lance, are 'merely' a sublimation of suppressed libido.

The insight that human consciousness is bounded by three thresholds, each permeable to different extents, in different ways and with different effects, allows us to start making sense of the correspondences between what is experienced beyond the 'light of common day' in each realm of extended awareness. Using Christian vocabulary, we could say that the forces embedded in our organism below the Inner Threshold, which regulate our bodily rhythms and also our instincts, drives and energy, arise in the realm of 'the Father'—the creator God who breathes life into nature and human nature. At the opposite pole, those intuitions, inklings and communications that we are sometimes able to perceive from beyond the Outer Threshold can be seen as glimpses and messages from the 'Holy Spirit', the Comforter who 'has yet much to reveal' to us. Between these, the Third Threshold allows us access to the sphere of love between human beings where the healing forces of the Son are active, leading us through the rhythms of sympathy, antipathy and empathy to the potential for seeing the Divine in the other person.

Just as, in Christian theology, the three Persons of the Trinity are also a unity, a three-in-oneness, so also this perspective on the three thresholds reveals them as three points of access to what is ultimately a single reality. To put it somewhat poetically, the three windows of the soul open in different directions, but through them we see different aspects of the same landscape. From this perspective, there is no need to choose between psychoanalytical and religious interpretations of mystical experiences, nor to assign the dynamics of relationships ultimately to either the biological or the doctrinal realm. Forces and opportunities from beyond all of the three thresholds play into every relationship, making each one unique.

The experience of falling in love can be so powerful and ecstatic—or devastating—because it carries us beyond ourselves in what Scott Peck calls 'a sudden and temporary collapse of the ego-boundaries'.[13] The Third Threshold seems almost to disappear, in the experience of merging and unification with the beloved. The confines of our everyday self seem to vanish: this could perhaps be compared to near-death experiences at the Outer Threshold, or the 'little death', as the French call it, of orgasm mediated by physiological processes across the Inner Threshold. The imagery of romantic love is never far from that of religion, involving for example courtship rituals, special places sacred to the relationship, icons, precious objects, and symbolism such as

---

[13] M. Scott Peck, *The Road Less Travelled*, Simon & Schuster, 1978 (Touchstone, 2003).

that of the never-ending form of the ring, betokening endless devotion. But as Peck also points out, the experience of 'in-loveness' cannot last forever (though we might, so as not to become too disillusioned, claim that it can be repeatedly recaptured, even with the same partner...), any more than ecstatic mystical experiences, or the intensity of orgasm, can be sustained indefinitely. The ego-boundaries snap back into place and we fall inevitably, sooner or later, into the realm of antipathy and separateness, even tension or conflict with our partner.

This is where the clichés about 'having to work on a relationship' find their validity. A partnership that relies mainly on automatic sympathy, plus sexual attraction, is unlikely to prove robust. Sooner or later, our lover will not seem quite so worthy of unconditional worship. The disappointment of falling out of love can be as devastating as the earlier infatuation, or more so. Somehow, an enduring partnership must embrace separateness as well as unity.

> When a man gets married, he assumes that his wife will remain as she is—and she doesn't.
> When a woman gets married, she assumes that her husband will change—and he doesn't...
>
> source unknown

Dependency and autonomy

'If your aim is to be loved,' Scott Peck tells us, 'you will never succeed.' This statement seems rather disheartening at first reading—most of us want, indeed need, to feel loved—but reveals an important paradox. The more we seek to be loved, to gain love from others as a benefit to ourselves, the less lovable, and the less worthy of love, we become. The need to be loved acts as an ulterior motive in all our interactions, subtly undermining the value, perceived and actual, of our acts of love towards others. But most of us are at least partially dependent on receiving as well as giving love in our relationships.

So how much dependency, mutual or otherwise, is healthy? I once spoke about this to a Swiss psychiatrist, who was insistent that dependency of any kind is a negative element in a marriage or partnership, something to be avoided or overcome as far as possible. A different psychiatrist, however, told me that 'whenever there is a sexual relationship, there is always dependency'. My own experience, and at least a superficial logic, tends to support this latter opinion. If sex is a general, if not universal, human need, then a monogamous relationship means, by definition, that one is dependent on one's partner for the fulfilment of that need (leaving aside Woody Allen's endorsement of masturbation as 'sex with someone I love'...). At a somewhat deeper level, the connection between the sexual and the emotional, and hence between the Inner Threshold and the interpersonal threshold, also connects sexual dependency and emotional dependency.

This is where the dangers arise, to which the first psychiatrist pointed. My partner may be a wonderful source of support, comfort, warmth, reassurance, confirmation, feedback, stimulus and satisfaction to me; but the more I *need* these from her, the more I 'cannot live without her', the less independent I become or remain. Arguably, highly dependent relationships keep people immature. Most of us know couples where the 'sacrifices' made by one or both partners for the sake of the relationship seem to arise more from insecurity and neediness than genuine altruism. The results in such situations often seem to include a limiting of potential personal development. In terms of threshold phenomena, this pattern involves an inhibition of the antipathy-forces: in a dependent relationship, separateness, difference, disagreement, withdrawal are felt as 'not OK', even as disloyal. Antipathetic impulses become sources of anxiety and are correspondingly suppressed.

Sometimes, the inter-dependencies in a relationship seem relatively balanced, though it is often an unstable balance. More often, one partner seems to be the stronger with the other more anxious and dependent. Below the surface, however, the apparently more assertive partner may be highly dependent on the other's dependency. Feeling needed is a seductive source of satisfaction. Wanting to be needed is a common and natural tendency for most of us; but it can become another form of dependency in itself. The provider role in a family—whether as protector, income-earner or homemaker—can be addictive and can trap people into a cycle of needing others to need them.

The dangers of such patterns for the individuals concerned are obvious. Not only may the dynamics of the relationship limit the extent to which people can explore their potential and extend their repertoire of expression and engagement, but if the relationship for any reason comes to an end, the consequences may be shattering. Paradoxically, this may cause more difficulties for the 'stronger' partner than the previously 'weaker', for whom the breaking of the dependency-cycle, even if imposed on them against their will, can quite soon prove to have been a liberation.

Craig had a powerful intellect and a powerful physique. Though not exactly handsome, he was found strongly attractive by a series of women who admired his confidence and air of authority. He had many opinions, expressed them forcefully, and took no prisoners in discussion. He was successful professionally and quickly became quite wealthy, despite the costs of divorce and child support, which he negotiated effectively to his own advantage.

His one weakness was that he did sometimes fall in love with a woman before trying to dominate her. Finally, one of these women left him rather than continue to be mistreated— an event he had never experienced or expected to experience. It threw him into crisis and the kind of depression he had always regarded scornfully in others. The woman, however, built a new life in a different country, started a new profession, and discovered strengths and potential in herself that had previously been locked deep inside.

The dependency dilemma brings us back to the issue of individualization described at the beginning of this book. As self-determination becomes more and more important to more and more people, the challenge of building durable partnerships becomes greater. From inner-city estates to royal palaces, relationship breakdown appears endemic. Experiments with open marriage and the prevalence of cohabitation before or instead of marriage have not provided consistent solutions. A substantial counselling and therapy industry has developed, to help people cope with and learn from relationship problems. Thousands of books claiming to provide answers have been written and sold. What can threshold-insights contribute to this vexed question?

In Part III of this book we will explore the inescapable reality of interdependence in the economic realm. None of us today can meet our own physical needs: we rely on the work of countless other people to provide what we need for bodily survival and comfort. Also on the level of the soul, we must admit that independence is an illusion, unless we abstain from relationships altogether. Sympathy and antipathy work in us continually: although we may choose to cultivate empathy, and become more conscious of our soul-processes, the soul itself is not free and will never be independent. Just as free decisions can only be made by an element of the human being which 'stands above' soul-phenomena—an element which we termed the individuality or self-conscious Ego—so only this element can be or become truly independent. What is commonly called ego—our self-image, self-will, self-ish longings, vanities and illusions—traps us in unhealthy dependency. This means that my two psychiatrists were both right, in different ways. Dependency, of body and soul, cannot and should not be avoided in intimate relationships; at the same time, the independence of the individuality must be sacrosanct.

D. H. Lawrence's *Women in Love*[14] is perhaps the quintes-sential novel of the Third Threshold. It explores the dynamics of family, friendship, sex and love in compelling narrative and dialogue. Often Lawrence himself seems to speak through the mouth of one of the main characters, Birkin, who decries the conventions of 'hunting in couples' and resists the 'merging' imagery of romantic love. He tells Ursula Brangwen that what he is seeking in their relationship is 'a strange conjunction with you ... not meeting and

---

[14] D.H. Lawrence, *Women in Love*, Penguin, 1995.

mingling ... but an equilibrium, a pure balance of two beings—as the stars balance each other'.

Perhaps what Lawrence was suggesting in this striking image, and what he strove to define, often by its absence, in much of his work, is close to the challenging ideal of a full, yet free, relationship. Unconditional, unrestrained engagement and commitment on the levels of body and soul, but complete individual autonomy on the spiritual level (not that DHL would have used that language) is what Birkin, Ursula and some of his other main characters—those few of whom he seems to approve—are searching for. Later in the book, he describes this as: '...a lovely state of free proud singleness, which accepts the obligation of the permanent connection with others, and with the other, submits to the yoke and leash of love, but never forfeits its own proud individual singleness, even while it loves and yields'.

Intimacy and individualism

A marriage vow:

I will be a faithful partner to your body
I will be a warm companion to your soul
I will honour and uphold the freedom of your spirit

There is no formula for building a healthy love-partnership, no simple checklist that can be applied. Intimacy in the age of individualism is a new challenge in the history of mankind: historical models will help us to only a limited extent. History, in fact, can be seen as one of the main obstacles to meeting this challenge. Although most contemporary societies have left behind the times when wives were seen as the property of their husbands, a dead weight of assumptions and expectations from the past still lies upon the whole field of love and partnership. Gender stereotypes are an obvious example: but the reaction against traditional roles can sometimes seem almost as unfree as conformity to them. It is difficult to be sure that our choices are made on the basis of genuine individual autonomy, in the light of external realities, and not out of past conditioning or an 'automatic' rebellion against such conditioning.

Modern sexology tries to overcome guilt and blame in relationships by stating that 'everyone is responsible for their own orgasms'. Equally, one could justifiably maintain that 'everyone is responsible for their own feelings', but neither of these statements frees us from sexual or emotional dependency on, or responsibility towards, our partner. The one realm where we can strive for full self-responsibility is that in which we exercise our own inner freedom. When we make moral choices, or embark on a path of self-development, we may do so with the support of our partner, but it must be support without interference. Developing the capacity to discern the boundary between the soul-realm of mutual influence, and the spiritual realm of individual freedom, seems fundamental to being able to orientate ourselves in the new territory of full and free partnership. A habit of differentiating between 'yours, mine and ours' within the relationship can be helpful. This simple formulation can be applied to possessions, money, tasks and needs between partners; but also to decisions and choices. Whichever of these has not been agreed as joint, must be respected as individual. This can be extremely challenging, especially when we see our partner about to make what we judge to be a rash or unwise decision. Treating them as an independent adult, however, means being available for consultation and trusting that they will let us know when they want to avail themselves of our wisdom...

We cannot often choose our feelings, but we can, in principle, choose how we handle them. When we become caught in a spiral of conflict with our lover or spouse, there will be moments when we can choose whether to escalate matters, to capitulate, or to try to change the dynamic into something more constructive. When we have lost control and behaved badly, we can choose whether, when, and how to apologize. When we feel let down by our partner, we can choose whether to suppress and hide our feelings, to express them in tones of resentment and blame, or to communicate how we feel in a way which allows our partner to understand the consequences of their actions or words without becoming defensive. All of these are individual decisions, to be made with as much inner freedom as we can muster amid the turbulent forces of strong emotion. They are acts of will by the individuality, the 'higher' Ego. Such acts of personal freedom are constantly playing into the dynamics of our relationships. Paradoxically, it seems that the more intimate the relationship, the more fundamental and existential it is in our lives, the more essential is this field of independence. If it is stifled or sidelined by the intensity of the love-dynamic, then sooner or later the relationship will suffer: one partner will tire of 'self-sacrifice' and need to break free from its constraints; or the other will get bored with the repetition of predictable patterns; or both will settle for comfort and compromise rather than continuing to explore the passionate potential of being together.

Only what remains separate can bring renewal and

development into what is built up together. When two people who are both on a self-conscious path towards inner freedom make a commitment to pursue a growing intimacy whilst also fully respecting each other's autonomy, then the fruits of individual development can flow into what weaves between them; their 'sleeping-into' each other can be consciously balanced by 'waking' withdrawal and reflection; a reliable and renewable empathy can develop; and the three thresholds can all be explored and extended in love on every level.

The Angel and Double of a relationship

Sometimes, over time, a relationship which is existentially important for the partners can seem almost to take on a life of its own, becoming a kind of third personality which influences the experience and life-orientation of the individuals. It is as if something has emerged or been born out of the dynamic between the two souls: in childless couples this phenomenon can sometimes be especially pronounced, but it can also be observed in large, close families. This 'relationship being' is nourished by the daily dynamics of interaction, and can be seen in a kind of collective culture which guides the individuals' behaviour when they are together, though they may each behave quite differently when they are away from each other.

In Chapter 5, the section entitled 'Meeting the shadow' included a description of the often shocking experience of encountering the Double of another person, with all its untransformed, unacknowledged negative characteristics. The opposite image, for which one could use the term 'Angel', represents the higher, positive potential in each person. In the 'relationship being' which arises between partners, one can also perceive a dark and a light side. The Angel of one couple's relationship, for instance, may appear as creative, open, enthusiastic and tolerant: the Double, however, when it suddenly becomes visible, may be a wild, chaotic, irresponsible being that respects no boundaries, and creates inner and outer turmoil for the partners and those close to them. Another family may develop a culture which, at its best, is disciplined, sincere and principled, but underneath, hidden and denied, there may be repressive, inhibiting forces which hinder the self-expression of the individual members.

One important characteristic of the Double, both on the individual and the relationship levels, is that it cannot be eliminated, only transformed. For this to happen, it must first be recognized: not in a spirit of guilty confession, but out of compassion. Both the Double and the Angel become visible at thresholds: in the case of the individual, at the Inner and Outer Thresholds respectively. The dark and light beings of a relationship appear at the Third Threshold. What might this mean for the way in which we handle and care for the relationships that are central in our lives? One implication is that whereas individuals can take personal responsibility and undertake personal self-development initiatives to work on their own shadow, the being of a relationship can only be addressed jointly. It is a product of the dynamic between the partners, and must be a shared responsibility. My partner and I have brought this being into the world, and must take responsibility for its impact on each of us and on others— especially our children, if we have any. We need to nurture it, guide it, periodically re-enliven it, sometimes work to transform or heal aspects of it which have become unhealthy.

A first challenge is whether we are able to talk about it. When the unhealthy aspects of our relationship become uncomfortably visible, can we move beyond mutual accusation or defensiveness and look together, with compassion, at the shortcomings and suffering of the Being we have brought into being? Can we also sometimes catch a glimpse of our relationship Angel and its ability to inspire us, to bring out the best in us, as it perhaps did in the early days of being together? Can we make these patterns and potential visible to each other, so that we can work together on what needs to be strengthened or changed?

It does sound like hard work: so many Beings to be looked after—you, me, the kids, the in-laws, the dog, the hamster, and now the Relationship Being as well... But every relationship is also an enrichment (which may be why we have the hamster...).

Confrontation without conflict; support without collusion

'Nowhere does Shakespeare portray a happy marriage', claimed Ian McKellen in a one-man show many years ago. He invited the audience to contradict him, and we all thought hard but could not come up with much. (Of course, many of Shakespeare's plays end with the *expectation* that the central couple(s) will live happily together in the future, but that future will only arrive, literally, after all the drama is over.) 'The Macbeths!' someone shouted, to general hilarity. Certainly there was an intense relationship between the murderous couple, and a kind of mutual support, but this was in the service of their common ruthless ambition, causing harm and death to others and ultimately destroying them both.

How can we provide consistent support for our partners, without colluding with their less noble actions and attributes? How can we confront what we may see as wrong or misguided, without damaging the relationship? Here again the sympathy/antipathy polarity arises, with all its challenges and dilemmas. On the one side, our commitment to the relationship, our affections and many of our own needs (for harmony, acceptance, warmth and so on) pull us towards a 'my partner right or wrong' orientation, which values solidarity above honesty and perhaps ultimately above morality.

Most of us have known 'cosy couples' between whom this kind of dynamic lives. Sometimes the public show of harmony contrasts with what happens behind closed doors, but often the reluctance to acknowledge tensions and differences, in front of the children, or otherwise, pervades the common culture of the partnership. When this happens, day to day living can be easier on the surface, but suppressed issues can fester unaddressed. Perhaps even worse, the personal development of the individuals is not stimulated by the challenge of disagreement or disapproval. 'There was nothing wrong with our marriage, until she left me . . .' was the plaintive claim of one abandoned husband. Of course, it cannot realistically have been true, but the statement is indicative of the self-deception which an artificially harmonious relationship can induce.

Somehow this kind of dysfunction in a relationship seems slightly old-fashioned today, though it is undoubtedly still widespread. More common, or at least more commonly visible, is its opposite: couples who speak (or sometimes scream) their differences at the slightest provocation. In the name of self-expression, openness, directness or honesty,

critical feedback is given free reign. In this mode, I feel free—
even obliged—to give my partner the benefit of my perceptions on everything they do 'wrong'; to point out every
manifestation of their vanity, hypocrisy, incompetence,
insensitivity, ignorance and so on. Usually, my continual
opportunities for observation at close quarters mean I am able
to find plenty of material for such pronouncements.

Some relationships are strong enough to sustain this kind
of pressure; but when it becomes continual or extreme, such
a pattern is usually the cause, or a symptom, or both, of
impending crisis. Paradoxically, intense fighting between
couples can often be a sign that the relationship is also intense
and existentially important; which does not mean that it is
viable in its current form, but it does mean that something
genuinely valuable is at stake, and at risk. Conflicts, of course,
have a tendency to escalate, often with highly damaging
consequences both for the protagonists and for those around
them.

Wherever there is potential conflict in a relationship, and
this means more or less every significant relationship in our
lives, we are faced with the tricky task of navigating between
unproductive avoidance on the one hand, and dangerous
confrontation on the other. What might a Third Threshold
perspective contribute to this dilemma?

In Chapter 9 the image of 'loving antipathy' was used to
describe an approach to reviewing and working to transform
influences from the subconscious. Something of the same
quality, it seems to me, is what we need to mobilize in dealing
with the problems of conflict and collusion in our relationships. Usually, our antipathy-forces serve our own purposes:
they keep us awake, protect us from being unduly influenced

or exploited, help us focus, reflect, keep in touch with our own sense of identity. In this context, though, the challenge is to *place our antipathy in the service of our partner*. When they do or say something that we experience as wrong, unwise, unfair or merely irritating, and we decide not simply to ignore it, we need to catch and re-balance our antipathy before expressing it. Our perception of the error or shortcoming is only one element of what is needed. The other is the sympathetic imagination of what needs to be heard, rather than what needs to be said. The crucial difference is the switch from the self-orientation of 'I'm holding this nugget of insight', to the other-orientation of 'How can I make my insight available in a way that is helpful to my partner?' Easier said than done, especially when my own needs are also involved.

Let's take a trivial example. Like many men, I have the annoying habit of leaving used crockery in the wrong place around the house. My wife decides that for her own sake and mine, it would be good to draw my attention to this. Her options might include saying things like:

- I'm sick of clearing away your dirty cups!
- Didn't your mother teach you to put things away after you've used them?
- Could you please try to remember to clear up after yourself?
- The children will never learn to be tidy if you don't set a better example.
- I always clear away my stuff, why can't you do the same?
- That's the fourth time today I've cleared up after you ...

... and so on. Her problem is that however right she may be (and she is) she risks coming across as nagging, petty, critical, intolerant, or even unloving. I might react defensively, coldly, irritably. I might feel hurt. Even if I acknowledge her point and comply with the request, I might do so resentfully. The atmosphere between us might be damaged, even if only slightly and temporarily. Many a relationship breakdown has begun with an inability to deal with such trivial issues. Is it worth even trying?

Fortunately for both of us, she is highly skilled in Third Threshold navigation. She knows that being right is not enough—indeed, it can even be dangerous because of the temptations (point-scoring, power-gaining, superiority and so on) to which it can give rise. Mildly but firmly, she remarks: 'You know, I can put your coffee cup in the dishwasher ... or you can.' There is no need to press the point, or to score points. The situation is clear, and I am left to draw my own conclusions about what needs to change. I feel slightly ashamed, but not humiliated or attacked. She has expressed the problem, but also her confidence in my ability to react appropriately once I see it.

Commitment without compulsion

What does it mean, in the twenty-first century, to commit to a relationship, to a partner? We have all attended weddings at which people make promises that they sooner or later fail to keep, or decide to reverse, or are unable to sustain. We are surrounded by single parents, blended families, individuals who are regretful or relieved refugees from failed relationships. The number of people who continue to get married, often more than once, can seem to represent the triumph of hope over experience. How realistic is it, actually, to make such commitments, in the light of all the changes of feeling, personal development, life-circumstance, new opportunities that are certain to follow?

Indeed, what is it that we are committing to? Our partner will change, we will change, in body and soul, so that we may well come to feel that neither of us is the same person we were at the start of the relationship. By promising permanence, are we locking ourselves into a contract which permanently restricts our future freedom? If I am truly bound by the promise, I am by definition not free to break it. Or if I retain this freedom, what is the point of making it in the first place, and, how can I rely on my partner's commitment if they remain free to change their mind at any time?

Nevertheless, many of us long for continuity and commitment, even if we repeatedly fail to sustain it. Commitment is an act of will; if the will is to remain free, the act must be continually renewed. It is future-directed; it cannot be compelled or constrained by the past. All that I can honestly and realistically state is my intention: that is the meaning of 'I will'. A statement of intent is not the same as a binding contract: however, it is not nothing, especially if it is made in good faith, after sound consideration and self-examination, and especially if it is made in the knowledge that the person I am committing to, and I myself, are realities beyond the fluctuations of soul and body. Rudolf Steiner expresses this beautifully in the following passage:

> Create for yourself a new and strongly courageous image of faithfulness. What people usually call faithfulness fades away so quickly. You however should make this into your faithfulness:
>
> You will experience fleeting moments with the other person, in which they appear as if filled and irradiated

by their essential spirit. And then there may, indeed will, come other moments, long periods in which people become darkened. You however should learn to say to yourself in such times: The spirit makes me strong. I shall think of the essence. I did see it once. No deception, no appearances shall rob me of it. Wrestle always for the image that you saw. This wrestling is faithfulness. And striving in this way for faithfulness, human beings will be close to each other, as if with the strength of guardian angels.

III

THE THIRD THRESHOLD
AT WORK

8. The Customer–Supplier Threshold

In supporting a process improvement project in a pensions company, I am struck by the commitment and empathic concern of the staff for their clients. The Customer Reps and junior managers are mostly in their twenties, living young single lives, and typically into sport, fashion, drinking etc. They are not particularly well paid. They deal daily with elderly pensioners and bereaved relatives, with whom one might imagine they have little in common, but in the course of the project they come up with a whole range of ideas for improving the service, the documentation, and the products, to meet these customers' needs more fully. What is more, they do this not mainly on the instructions of their managers, but because it genuinely motivates them.

In the first part of this book I tried to describe and explore the general phenomena of the social or relational threshold, as a way of understanding and working with the challenges and opportunities which relationships of all kinds offer us. In the second part, we looked at how the 'archetypal social phenomenon' shows itself in the most intimate relationships in our lives. In this section, we will examine the implications for the world of work of our key themes so far, namely:

- community and individuation
- the soul-forces of thinking, feeling and will
- sympathy and antipathy, sleeping and waking
- invasion and deprivation

- trust and distrust
- the cycle of perceptions, attitudes and behaviour
- empathy and the shadow

In the opening chapter of Part I, mention was made of the ongoing historic transition from a power-based to a bargaining society. Of course, power—of governments, corporations, classes and individuals—still plays an enormous role in our lives, but more and more of the decisions which affect us today are based on negotiated transactions of one kind or another: between nations, between both public sector and commercial organizations, between employers and unions, between managers and staff, and between customers and suppliers of all kinds.

Whatever scale of organization the individuals are representing, negotiation always takes place between human beings. That is to say, it is a process which moves back and forth across the Third Threshold.

'Customers are from Venus, suppliers are from Mars' (George Perry)

Customer–supplier negotiations are concerned with an *exchange of value*—usually, though not always, the value of goods and/or services against the value of money. For sellers, this means that understanding the values of customers is fundamental to success. Values are subjective, not always rational—they are a reality on the feeling level of the psyche. Because of this, there is clearly a role for empathy here, but it can be a problematic one. If I try to practise and demonstrate empathy towards my clients, will they interpret this as manipulation? Do my ulterior motives (wanting to make or repeat a sale) compromise the genuineness of my concern for their needs? Typically, potential customers tend to feel invaded by suppliers (adverts, junk mail, cold-calling, pushy sales people...), where suppliers often feel deprived by customers, their efforts and offers disregarded. In terms of the archetypal social phenomenon, sellers may be using sympathy in the attempt to put the other person to sleep—and prospective customers will therefore react with antipathy to keep themselves awake.

Customers: can't live with them, can't live without them...

My colleague receives a request from a potential client for some help with an organizational issue. She visits, writes notes of the conversation and together we formulate a proposal. The client asks for some further information, which we provide, then a teleconference at which he states that the proposal is 'spot on' and he will refer it internally for approval. For some weeks we hear nothing, in spite of the stated urgency of the original request. When we gently enquire about progress, we are told that the requirements have changed somewhat, and another meeting to discuss them is arranged. This time we both attend, have an apparently productive conversation, and I write up some notes outlining a revised approach which seemed to be agreed. Again, no response for several weeks. 'A supplier would never treat us like that,' my colleague remarks, 'or they wouldn't be a supplier for long...'

One reason for the typical resistance of customers to the chat-up routines and blandishments of sellers may be the common experience of poor after-sales service. Once the conquest is made and the contract signed, the seller, like an unscrupulous seducer, becomes indifferent, fails to follow through with the promised commitment, and moves on to the next prospect; thus reversing the deprivation experience of unsuccessful wooing.

Service, commitment and purchasing power

The best customer–supplier relationships, like the best personal relationships, are based on mutual commitment, in which both sides genuinely seek to optimize and balance the benefits of the transactions. This means customers resisting the temptation to exploit their (pre-purchase) financial power, and suppliers ensuring that every stage of the sale–supply–consumption cycle is reliably satisfying for their customers. Empathy on both sides is required here, and a willingness to take risks in order to build trust. The pursuit of narrow, short-term self-interest can only lead to a pattern of mutual exploitation, in which the costs of self-protection limit the overall value of the relationship.

A key quality for the supplier to cultivate is *authenticity*: there is simply no substitute for genuine concern for customer needs. It is remarkable how easy it is, as a customer, to discern whether the person serving you is truly interested in meeting your needs, or whether they have just been trained to *appear* to be so. Our ability to cross the Third Threshold and experience imaginatively the soul-reality of the other is uncannily acute in perceiving pretence. Negotiators who are inclined to duplicity are often quite naïve in their assumptions about the naïvety of their intended victims.

Can you trust a used car salesman?

In trying to agree a price for a car I like at a local garage, I conscientiously apply the negotiation techniques which I have taught to hundreds of managers: I prepare well, gather information on comparable vehicles, assess my fall-back options, try to cultivate a constructive relationship, and resist the temptation to make counter-offers. I tell the salesman that if we can agree a price, I'll give him a deposit immediately. He keeps lowering the price incrementally, between multiple cups of coffee and trips to the back office to consult his boss before making further concessions. Finally we reach a sticking point, where I still feel he might come down a little further if I hold out. Then he pulls off a master stroke: he fetches the garage's purchase ledger and shows me what they paid for the car I'm interested in. 'Look, Mr Briault,' he says, 'how much profit do you think we should make on this vehicle?' I'm taken aback by his openness, and feel turned inside-out by his question. To respond, I need to consider the needs of his business as well as my own interests. 'Well,' I think, 'you've got premises here to maintain, salaries, overheads ... I guess if you don't make a margin of ten per cent or so, you'll be in trouble...'. At that moment it becomes clear to both of us what a fair price would be: we agree it, I pay the deposit, and we shake hands in mutual satisfaction.

Was I conned? Cynics to whom I have told the story joke about the 'special purchase ledger', but my empathetic sense at the time was that he was genuine. I will never know for certain, but does it matter, if I'm happy with the deal I got?

The Double of the supplier is the con man, who ingratiates himself, exaggerates the value of whatever snake-oil he is selling, and disappears as soon as he has been paid. It is rare to meet a supplier who has absolutely none of this tendency.

When we are ourselves in the seller/supplier role, one of the most constructive things we can do to keep our relationships with customers healthy, is to examine our own attitudes and behaviours critically in order to diagnose and control this pattern in ourselves.

Conventional economic thinking tells us to maximize our own interests by giving as little as possible in return for as much as possible. Yet paradoxically, the thoroughgoing application of this principle leads to an impoverished economic life of mutual exploitation, in which relationships are merely instrumental and every participant is justly suspicious of every other.

'Delivering real value for customers creates joy in the supplier' (Brian Swain)

The old wooden farmhouse in the Vorarlberg which we have rented for our holiday is everything we could wish for—picturesque, cosy, convenient, well equipped, and surrounded by stunning landscape. Even more striking than this, however, is the careful consideration with which our needs have been provided for. The landlady meets us at the station and takes us to the house, makes up the beds as we want them, and modestly shows us what she has prepared: right-sized bikes for each family member (including a seat for the toddler); ping-pong table with good bats and a new box of balls; barbecue, charcoal, and fire-lighters; garden furniture and umbrella; a stable full of ready-cut firewood for the traditional ceramic stove, whose use she demonstrates. Halfway through our stay, a neighbour calls to check we have all we need, and pick up our bag of rubbish to put out for collection. All this for half the price of one hotel room per night...

The fact of being paid does not preclude acting altruistically: the experience of the transaction will in fact be more satisfying (and therefore more profitable) for *both* parties if the supplier focuses not primarily on the money they will receive, but on maximizing the value they can create for customers. Payment can then be seen as a necessary enabler to allow this value to continue to be produced.

The empathy of suppliers for customers is, at least initially, driven by self-interest: but what can drive empathy in the other direction? Why should customers worry about the needs of suppliers, beyond paying the minimum price available? The Double of the customer is the slave-driver, demanding ever more and more for less and less. In recent years, Western industry has come round to an awareness of the long-term dysfunctionality of this approach: suppliers who are pressed too hard go out of business or find ways of cutting corners, creating a lose/lose cycle for themselves and their customers. To avoid this, most businesses now espouse the logic—or at least the rhetoric—of partnership with their suppliers. Paying lip-service to this idea is of course not enough, however: habitual attitudes and behaviours born of decades of adversarial relationships need to be fundamentally transformed.

From transaction to partnership

Two finance companies I worked with were both part of the same supply chain for a large number of end customers. In the various processes involved, they were both customers and suppliers to each other. Relationships and operational performance had been poor for some time, with a lot of mutual criticism. Their record-keeping and tracking systems were not aligned, and the constraints of existing technology on both sides made it hard even to agree what the current situation was regarding backlog, error rates, etc.

When they finally agreed to undertake a facilitated joint improvement project, some preconditions had to be established before productive work could begin. Senior management support from both organizations was essential. The provision of hospitality at each other's offices (echoes of the Beast's castle . . .) helped warm things up. Negotiation of resources for the project already required a degree of mutual commitment. After an initial period of 'blamestorming', an agreed list of issues to be addressed was drawn up. Then began the painstaking process of creating an understanding of each other's ways of working—entering foreign territory across the organizational threshold, suspending judgements, moving from 'Why can't you just . . .' to 'What if we. . .'.

At the end of each meeting, the teams returned to their base to reflect on what had been learned, and to prepare for the next round—taking the outcomes of a sympathy-driven process back into the antipathy of separateness, from the warmth of collaboration to the cold light of self-interest, to questions of feasibility, cost/benefit calculations, implementation issues. Gradually, over a series of meetings and interim work, the profile of a joint future state process emerged and was agreed, guided by the needs of the end customers whom both organizations served. The elimination of delay and waste, through better alignment, allowed a win/win/win outcome, but continuing vigilance and effort will be needed in the future, to keep this threshold transparent and permeable.

In the attempt to create a culture of real partnership, people have to confront the boundary issues mentioned in Chapter 4—especially the semi-automatic tendency to blaming and defensiveness which arises whenever there are tensions or differences of interest between organizational units. The perceptions–attitudes–behaviour cycle needs to be made conscious on both sides of the relationship. Often, considerable tact, skill, courage, and commitment are required to build the trust needed for open communication, joint problem-solving and collaborative development.

The great paradox of economic life is this: in order for markets to work, both customers and suppliers must act in their own self-interest; however, in order for overall value to be maximized, all parties need to 'expand their egoism'—not in the sense of becoming more egoistic, but in the sense of becoming more *inclusive* in the considerations which are taken into account in decision-making. It needs to be seen not as naïve idealism, but as enlightened long-term self-interest, to be concerned with the interests of transaction partners, the wider community, and the earth itself, as well as with our own immediate needs, in the deals we do.

'The paradox of the modern world is this: We have never been more *interdependent* in our needs; and we have never been more *individualist* in our outlook.'

Speechwriter for Tony Blair, October 2002

9. The Management/Leadership Threshold

In the relationships within an organizational hierarchy, the 'political' element of power plays its part alongside the economic element of bargaining. Although the content of the work and the purpose of the organization may be externally focused, towards the needs of clients, patients, students, and so on, the internal relationships play a crucial role in driving or inhibiting performance, as well as in affecting the experience of the workforce. The aspect of formal authority creates an 'above and below' dynamic in addition to the 'supply chain' phenomena which we have mainly discussed so far.

Co-ordination and subordination

The task of management is to co-ordinate the many factors of the work system, including the efforts of its people. Does co-ordination necessarily require sub-ordination? I once contested this with a colleague who claimed that it does. 'No', I argued, 'you and I can co-ordinate our diaries without either of us being subordinate to the other...'. Reflecting later, however, on the repeated frustrating experience of trying to co-ordinate arrangements with a group of peers, I can accept that he had a point. At a certain scale and level of complexity, one just wants someone to make a decision—and that someone has to carry authority in order for their decision to command (interesting word here!) acceptance and compliance.

Next, though, comes the question of consent. If our 'second

proposition' about individuation (Part I, Chapter 1) is cor-
rect, it will be (and already is) increasingly difficult for those
in authority to assume automatic obedience from their subordinates.

> A recent article in the Harvard Business Review carries the
> challenging title: *'Why Should Anyone Be Led By You?'* Its
> authors claim that posing this question is an excellent way to
> reduce a room full of senior executives to silence: 'Without
> fail, the response is a sudden, stunned hush. All you can hear
> are knees knocking.'[15]

Why this insecurity? Why the enormous market for pub-
lications, courses and research in the field of leadership
theory and practice? On the train, I sit next to a young
woman who is reading one of these books. Trying not to
be invasive, I sneak a look at the page she is on: it contains,
in the bold type of a section heading, the less-than-
astonishing revelation: 'Leadership happens between
people...' Why do we need to be told this? Perhaps
because recently a distinction has emerged between management and leadership, as two different though often not
divisible activities and skill-sets. The latter is often regarded
as more problematic than the former: most people can
learn to be a competent manager, the argument goes, but
the debate continues as to whether leaders are born or
made, and what attributes and skills they need. For our
purposes, the important issue is how what 'happens
between people'—the experience of the social threshold—
is affected by the dimension of positional power.

---

[15] R. Goffey and G. Jones, HBR, 2000.

> In some businesses, the organization chart, showing what a cynical colleague described as 'a Christmas tree with lots of branches and a fairy at the top, but no lights', is still referred to as 'the family tree'.
>
> A very experienced, matriarchically-inclined factory manager once told me that her way of leading change was to get people to 'hold tight to Mother's hand . . .'.

The relationship between leader and follower, manager and subordinate, carries a strong parental element. Good parents provide care, support, guidance, discipline, protection, and resources. They set a good example. They tell inspiring stories. They listen and try to empathize, even in the face of undesirable behaviour. Good leaders and managers do all of these things. However, the analogy is risky. Organizational subordinates are not children (even though they may some-times behave like them—an occasional tendency which also shows itself in managers . . .). The leadership prerogative of the manager is not inborn but contractual, and in day-to-day practice it requires conscious consent. Any suggestion of authoritarianism, in contemporary Western organizations, may provoke resistance or subversion. Unlike the parental remit, and unlike the situation in former historical periods, the hierarchical aspect of management is limited to the work context and does not extend to other areas of life. Nevertheless, the awareness of positional authority is ever-present in the interactions between most managers and their subordinates.

In terms of the social archetype, this seems to have an intensifying effect. Even though the manager may have a certain right, even duty, to intervene in the activities of subordinates, to feel invaded by someone in a more powerful position is even more uncomfortable, because less resistible, than feeling this from a peer. Equally, to feel ignored or unsupported by the person to whom you are professionally accountable can also be very debilitating. Potentially, this dynamic puts both parties in an invidious situation. As manager, I constantly run the risk of creating resistance by intervening too strongly, or resentment by seeming too distant. If I have a number of subordinates, I need to judge how much contact, of what kind, is appropriate for each one—both from the point of view of their individual well-being, and to promote the effectiveness of their work. As follower, I need to show respect and to ask for and receive support and guidance, without allowing myself to become subservient or over-dependent. I also need to preserve my self-respect, and sometimes set some boundaries to my boss's involvement, without creating conflict or offence, or appearing to be an awkward employee.

Clarity, empathy, energy—and trust

Building healthy relationships between managers/leaders and subordinates needs careful attention to the interactive dynamics of each of the thresholds—thinking, feeling and will—described in Part I, Chapter 3. All of these three need to be handled hygienically; otherwise any or all of them can become toxic, with corresponding impacts on relationships and work performance.

Clear communication

This should, on the face of it, be the easiest to achieve. Intellectual skills generally feature prominently, explicitly or implicitly, in the selection criteria for management posts; so one could expect those achieving promotion to command a significant level of proficiency and precision in the use of words and numbers. However, the managerial culture of reports, briefings, presentations, bullet points, and so on, can just as easily baffle as enlighten. *Stating* something clearly is not the same as *communicating* it effectively. The language, level of detail, and liveliness of illustration needs to be appropriate to the audience. Engagement is the essential precondition: as the email-footer cliché has it, *'People don't care how much you know, until they know how much you care.'* Regularly subjecting your staff to 'death by PowerPoint', even if done in the name of transparency and openness, will not necessarily create understanding. My management clients often tell me, with a degree of exasperation: 'We've told them again and again' (or sometimes: 'It's there on the Intranet'), 'but they still say they haven't been informed...'. However good we are at telling people things, they will always be better at resisting being told.

The simple reality is that information without an emotional or motivational dimension is often just dry and boring. The solution is to integrate the levels of feeling and will into one's communication practise—more on this later. However, even on the purely cognitive level, there are some simple principles and guidelines which can help to avoid confusion or switch-off.

Suggestions for improving staff communication on the 'head' level

1. Communicate face to face and informally wherever possible, with individuals or small groups. Use documents, presentations or data sparingly for illustration or where more detail is important;

2. Give information in small doses, with pauses between each dose to allow questions and check understanding;
3. Wherever possible, invite people to draw their own conclusions about the facts presented—then discuss your own interpretations alongside theirs;
4. Use open questions to stimulate people's thinking and engagement;
5. Use examples, stories, jokes, to illustrate and enliven your communication.

Warmth of feeling

Human warmth is the element that prevents work relationships from being purely instrumental. Without it, the manager becomes a cog in an organizational machine, turned by and turning other cogs with no regard for the joys and sufferings of subordinates, colleagues or superiors. A soulless workplace is the result—fortunately not as common, in my experience, as one might fear. Humans are relational beings, and even, or perhaps especially, when they are engaged in a mechanistic task, they have feelings about each other. Often, of course, these are the familiar feelings of sympathy and antipathy, liking and disliking, friendship and animosity. The manager or leader, however, cannot afford simply to participate in these dynamics. Not only is impartiality a prerequisite for legitimate authority; an effective leader must find a way of building at least a cordial, and preferably a genuinely warm relationship with every individual reporting to him/her, whether or not they feel an instinctive sympathetic connection with the person.

It is possible to *empathize* even with people one dislikes (cf. Part I, Chapter 5), and the capacity to do so is essential for effective and inspiring leadership. 'Why should anyone be led...', to adapt the title of the Harvard Business Review article mentioned above, '...by someone who is incapable of understanding how they feel, or unconcerned to try?'

Here especially, though, we encounter the invasion/ deprivation dilemma, the violation or avoidance of the Third Threshold, in an enhanced form. If I am going through a difficult time in my family life, do I want my manager's involvement, however supportive? Do I even want them to know about it, if it does not affect my work? Will I welcome sympathetic, or even empathetic, enquiries? Equally, if I am clearly troubled and my manager simply ignores this, what kind of leader, what kind of human being, are they?

Are there ways out of this apparent minefield? One important way is certainly to establish a relationship of warmth and openness from the outset, so that there is a supportive context for any issues which may subsequently arise. This can usually be done by the conscious, judicious, and progressive use of empathy from the early phase of the relationship.

Suggestions for improving staff communication on the 'heart' level

1. Show interest in the whole person, not just their skills and performance;
2. Try to sense the level of personal disclosure that the individual is comfortable with (this may change over time), and stay within it;
3. Be prepared to share some of your own feelings about both work and non-work situations, without assuming personal friendship or burdening people with unwanted intimacy;
4. Enquire discreetly about anything that may be affecting

people emotionally, without prying or analysing: a simple 'How are you feeling today?' is often enough to show concern, and allows people to answer in whatever way is right for them.

5. Don't offer advice on non-work issues unless you are sure it is wanted!

Good will

There are thousands of books and articles on how to motivate employees, and it is not intended to duplicate that material here, though reference will be made to some of it. The threshold question, however, is: How do I engage the will of my staff in our common tasks, without infringing their freedom? The language of sticks and carrots, so often and so tiresomely trotted out by managers of a certain kind, immediately fails this criterion. As Herzberg famously pointed out, if I kick my dog to make him move, it is I and not the dog who is motivated. The dog simply reacts to stimulus. In spite of the popular cartoon image, even donkeys will not walk all day in the hope of reaching the carrot dangled in front of them. The animal imagery is significant: behaviour modification using reward and punishment is a sub-human approach, which can never stimulate the free will of human beings, only their greed or fear.

Motivational skills are often looked for in leaders: but what is the concrete activity I am supposed to be engaged in, when I am motivating someone? If it is not to be merely a variant on carrot-dangling or stick-wielding, it must be an invitation, not a command or an inducement. Inspirational leaders, unlike 'transactional' leaders, offer a vision and an opportunity which people are free to connect with—or not. This freedom makes the difference between inspiration and ideology.

Our true motivation is arguably the deepest, most personal aspect of our soul-life: it is what expresses who we really are, what we want from the world and what we want to give to the world. No one else should determine this—if they try, they are attempting to steal a part of our essential identity. That is what makes manipulative advertising such a corrosive force in our culture. At the same time, because the will is the least conscious part of our soul (see Part I, Chapter 3), accessing it, even in ourselves, is problematic. As a manager, it is often tempting to think: They don't really know what they want, so I need to tell them...

What does a healthy approach to staff motivation look like? One important principle is that free, good will is only sustainable on the basis of engaging the other two soul-forces, so that people can choose to contribute their commitment and energy because they *understand* the needs they are serving (and why and how) and *feel* personally warm towards their task, their customers, their colleagues, and their leaders.

Beyond this, most of the research conducted around the theme of motivation seems to point to the importance of *recognition* as a key factor. Clearly, praise creates a feel-good factor which people respond to: however, if given too readily this can in the long run become little more than a sophisticated carrot, which loses its effect as it is taken for granted, but creates a negative effect if it is withdrawn. True recognition is more than giving compliments: it is a genuine expression of positive threshold-crossing. The traditional African greeting 'I see you' expresses much more than a hello: it is a recognition of the unique individuality of the other person. Somewhere we all long for such recognition. Managers can provide it only if they are able to make their staff members feel truly *seen*, by recognizing not only the outer contribution which has been made, but also the inner effort and development which made this possible.

10. The Collegial Threshold

Around two hundred books are produced every year in English on the theme of leadership, along with countless articles, training courses, development programmes, and coaching services. The questions: *What makes a good leader?* and *How do people become good leaders?* receive massive investment. However, very little if any attention is given to the—arguably just as important—issue of *colleagueship*. Organizations today are increasingly arranged on the basis of teamwork, and layers of management are kept to a minimum. This makes the quality of collaboration between peers in the workplace crucial to business success: yet the critical success factors for effective colleagueship have hardly been researched or articulated.

What qualities do people look for in their colleagues?

Intrigued by this question, an international group of colleagues and I conducted a modest piece of research, in which about four hundred people from twelve different countries including Russia, North America, Australia, Scandinavia, and Europe responded to a simple questionnaire. They were asked to rank twenty qualities in terms of how important each of them is as a positive attribute in their colleagues, and also to note the qualities they would like to develop further in themselves, to become better colleagues. The highest scores, in order of importance, were for:

1. Honesty, integrity
2. Reliability, accountability
3. Professionalism, competence
4. Collaborative, good team player.

Interestingly, 'Values and aims in common with me' was ranked quite low overall, whilst 'Warm, generous, kind' was also not a priority. 'Good at negotiation and conflict-handling' was rated fairly low, but was frequently mentioned as a self-development goal.

What does this tell us? If the sample was at all typical, it seems that what people most look for in colleagues is a solid moral and professional basis for collaboration. More personal and interpersonal aspects—though certainly not unimportant—seem to be secondary to these ethical and practical foundations.

How is good colleagueship built?

To be an effective team member, I must first gain the trust of my colleagues through demonstrating honesty, integrity and reliability. Secondly, I must ensure my own competence, and continuous development, for our common tasks. Then I must develop the specific skills of collaboration. These are distinct from the ones that belong to the leadership role: as a colleague, I cannot rely on the exercise of authority to influence my fellow workers. Amongst my peers, I need to understand the strengths and limitations of each person, and how to call on their resources without being able to direct them. I need to anticipate how they will react in different circumstances, and how to make myself available for them when they need my support. In meetings and conversations, I need to 'let go . . .', as Christian Schumacher puts it, of my own inputs to the discussion, '. . . in order that they can be transformed into other, better, team outputs'.

The archetype of the team is displayed dramatically in the animal world, in the way that creatures such as wolves or dolphins collaborate in hunting, or the remarkable selflessness shown by individual bees or ants for the benefit of their community. In human history, we can imagine it evolving from the hunter-gatherer societies, through the intense comradeship which develops, ironically enough, in the context of armed conflict, to the sublimation of conflict in the 'battlefields' of ball games where our modern imagery of teamwork is rooted. Good team players pass the ball, resisting the temptation to succeed personally at the expense of the team; share opportunities and achievements; encourage each other; and develop what Katzenbach and Smith in *The Wisdom of Teams* call 'a common approach'.[16] In this last little phrase, the potential for modern community-building in the workplace is hinted at. When a group of colleagues start to experience that by their commitment to their common goals and to each other, they have started to build a joint ethos or culture, a shared identity which is not inherited from the past but created out of their collaboration towards future-oriented aims, then each individual can feel part of something which is greater than themselves and more than the sum of its parts.

---

[16] Katzenbach and Smith, *The Wisdom of Teams: Creating the High-Performance Organization*, Harper Business, 2003.

Teambuilding Dispositions (adapted from Christian Schumacher)

For a group to become an effective team, its members must be prepared to:

1. proactively ensure their own competence for their task within the team, and constantly develop their own skills;
2. communicate openly with other team members, giving and seeking all appropriate information and feedback;
3. help and support the others, both morally and practically;
4. accept responsibility for the group's task as a whole, beyond their individual role within it;
5. enter into a two-way contract with the team leader, which acknowledges authority in return for the leader's commitment to the welfare and success of the team;
6. contribute their skills and ideas freely to the group, and be willing to let go of these inputs, to allow them to be transformed into (other, better) team outputs;
7. value, appreciate and enjoy the benefits of effective teamwork.

Key to the development of successful teamwork is the element of *mutual accountability*; members of a real team feel a responsibility to each other which is at least as strong as their responsibility to the boss. If one member fails to perform, the leader may be disappointed or angry, but this is not as important as the sense of having let one's colleagues down. Equally, the motivation to give of one's best comes just as much from the team context as from the external rewards or the quality of the leadership. In a workplace, it is usually quite easy to observe the difference between a boss-oriented and a team-oriented culture. In the latter, the temporary absence of the leader makes little if any difference to the productivity or creativity of the group. The image of the 'servant leader' reflects this—the formal leadership role is most effective when the team of colleagues say of their successes: 'We did it ourselves'.

11. Organizational Thresholds

The image of relationship between the logs in a fireplace, enabling or inhibiting the generation of warmth (p. 17), has implications for the design of teams and organizations. Structure—the way in which different parts are positioned in relation to each other—is an enabler or a disabler for the culture and performance of the whole. To use a different analogy, an effective team—in football, for example— needs the right degree of differentiation between the roles of the individual players, as well as the right degree of flexibility and mutual support. Each team member needs to understand their own 'position' and area of personal responsibility, and also be willing and able to adapt from moment to moment to the needs of the team as a whole. When defending a corner or free kick close to goal, the strikers will come back to help out. If the team is behind with very little time left, even the goalkeeper will some- times join the attack. On the other hand, if all the players constantly chase the ball, as kids playing sometimes do, the opportunity for effective passing will be lost. A good team will constantly keep its shape, retaining the integrity of its overall structure whilst also continually flexing roles to meet the necessities of the moment.

Organizational boundaries as designed thresholds

In organizations, the boundaries between individual roles and between workgroups or departments, are formal thresholds which need to be carefully designed and managed. They are like an externalized, objective set of Third Thresholds: at these interface points, we can see people thinking, feeling, and behaving in ways which mirror the phenomena that we have been exploring.

Although it used to be fashionable to talk about breaking down boundaries in management circles, it is now widely recognized that boundaries are necessary for effective organization. Without them, we would not have organizations, only crowds. The management issue is not whether to have boundaries or not, but how to get the boundaries in the right places, and how to ensure they have the right degree of permeability.

Boundaries bring people together, and separate people from each other. They create certain relationships, and inhibit others. This reality needs to be reflected in decisions about organizational design. Where people need to communicate and co-operate closely, it is best to avoid putting organizational boundaries between them. Conventional structures—based on function or profession— often fail to meet this principle. For example, a group of sales people may be placed under a sales manager and called a sales team: but in what sense are they really a team? Do they support each other, or in practice, compete with each other? Do they need each other to complete their tasks on behalf of the organization, or do they mostly act as lone wolves? Can they work as a team to deliver a complete service to customers, or does this need the collaboration of a whole set of others, such as delivery and service staff, administrators, and marketing professionals? Often, a team composed of people with the same function is actually like a team of goalkeepers—not a real team at all.

Where should organizational boundaries be placed, to create structures that best help people work together? The socio-technical answer is: 'At points of minimum inter-dependence', or, in plainer language, where they separate activities and people who do not need to co-operate closely, and bring together those who do. Christian Schumacher's 'Work Structuring' approach offers a set of principles and tools for organization and job design based on this way of thinking. For our purposes, the important point is that the realities of the Third Threshold need to be taken into account in the architecture of our organizations, just as the realities of physical forces and aesthetic considerations need to be acknowledged in the design of buildings. The structure needs to give individuals enough personal autonomy to encourage them to take responsibility and exercise creativity, at the same time as providing enough clarity of role and accountability to ensure alignment with the wider aims of the organization. Structures which are too tight will be experienced as stifling, while those which are too loose will prove confusing or exploitable.

Alienation and belonging

The phenomena of invasion and deprivation described in Chapter 4 are to be found on an organizational as well as individual level. If a workgroup is responsible only for low-level, non-value-adding tasks such as fetching and carrying, filing, packing and unpacking or clearing up, they can easily feel like 'slave groups' (Schumacher) who are constantly invaded and bossed around by higher-status people who do 'the real work' of the organization. Equally, a group whose efforts are frequently ignored or denigrated by the wider organization—back-office administrators are often in this situation—may feel deprived of recognition and reward, and become highly demotivated as a result.

People feel safe within a familiar physical and social environment. Belonging to a team, a department, a business unit, gives a sense of identity and security. Thresholds keep out the unfamiliar and the potentially threatening. This is why crossing them takes courage. The fear of otherness leads to isolation, self-enclosure, shrinking back from meeting; even though economic life increasingly demands communication and collaboration across all kinds of boundaries—national, organizational, professional, cultural. This tension poses a potentially constructive, developmental challenge in almost every workplace.

In my work in organization development, I have continually come across situations where people who serve the same customers, are part of the same production or service delivery process, have never met or spoken with each other. In many large hospitals, for example, the people who book patient appointments into the same clinic slots to see the same doctors, never meet: some of them work in a central call centre, often on a different site; some are medical secretaries; some are part of an outsourced booking service; some are clinic receptionists, and some are nurses within the hospital or general practitioners outside it, who have direct contact with patients. If all these different groups stay within their own organizational boundaries, the context is ripe for misunderstandings, confusion, duplication, rework, and mutual recrimination. Bringing them together to review the processes they all contribute to can be a challenging but very rewarding endeavour.

If organizational thresholds are put in the wrong place, they impede teamwork, to the ultimate detriment of the organization's customers. Inconsistent professional development paths, contrasting pay structures, contradictory performance measures, can all contribute to an unhealthy impermeability of the boundaries between people. Businesses which preach a culture of teamwork but reward managers for individual performance are a classic instance of this. To take another healthcare example, government targets for access to treatment can create conflict between clinicians and hospital managers: the targets only apply to new patients, so managers are incentivized to prioritize these over others who have started to receive treatment but need follow-up consultations. The doctors, by contrast, feel responsible for their patients, who are already part of their case-load, and might prefer to limit the number of new referrals so that they can give more attention to those already receiving care. No wonder that doctors and managers often feel themselves to be on different sides of the fence...

Organizations as mirrors of human nature

As God is said to have created mankind in His own image, so mankind creates organizations in its own image. Our communities, businesses, governments, and work groups reflect the nature of the human being in many ways. They have a growth and maturity cycle. They have a physical body, a kind of unique identity, and a soul often described as the specific culture of the organization. Like us as individuals, they have both positive and negative characteristics. They like to advertise their ideals and their strengths, and keep quiet about their vices and weaknesses, just as we do. They have relationships with other organizational personae that range from close collaboration to competition and conflict.

In a reflection of the Third Threshold experience, we may penetrate the boundaries of an organization in a variety of ways. One of them is to purchase its products and feel how much, or how little, they live up to the organization's self-presentation. It used to be said, only a little unfairly, that the name of the now-defunct airline Sabena was an acronym for 'Such A Bad Experience—Never Again. . .'. Genuinely high-quality organizations, on the other hand, provide better-than-anticipated experiences for their customers, leading to long-term relationships, just as good friendships offer deeper rewards than superficial attraction expects. Another way of penetrating an organization's threshold is to work for it, either as an employee or a contractor. When in one of these ways we go beyond its arty logo, its lofty mission statement, its advertising hype, and its product packaging, we may encounter both the Beauty and the Beast—the Angel and the Double—of the organization. Often, these two sides reflect their equivalent in the character of the founder. For example, Ford Motor Company still displays something of the virtues and flaws of the original Henry Ford: the rather fanciful idealism that expressed itself in his claim that motor vehicles were a force for reconciliation (because they enabled more people to travel around and meet each other) or in his attempts to stop the First World War (by hiring a ship, filling it with wise men and sending them across the Atlantic to persuade the European powers to cease hostilities); as well as the ruthlessness that turned the Ford Personnel Department, in the 1920s, into little more than a gang of thugs whose union-smashing activities often took quite brutal forms.

Teaching negotiation skills to managers in Ford in the 1990s, I felt I was still grappling with these two contradictory tendencies in the organization's culture and its founder.

In all these aspects of organizational design, development and management, Third Threshold intelligence is essential. Whether we are designing structures, orchestrating culture or trying to bring healing to the often conflict-ridden interface between different organizations, an appreciation of threshold phenomena and dynamics will be a decisive asset.

THE MEANING OF THE THIRD
THRESHOLD

12. Human relationships and human rights

In March 2009, a group of more than twenty different UN bodies warned that the world may be close to its first water war. 'Water is linked to the crises of climate change, energy and food supplies and prices, and troubled financial markets,' said the report. 'Unless their links with water are addressed and water crises around the world are resolved, these other crises may intensify and local water crises may worsen, converging into a global water crisis and leading to political insecurity and conflict at various levels.'

In the conclusion to his wide-ranging book, *Mankind and Mother Earth*,[17] the historian Arnold Toynbee writes of a recent (in the context of the broad historical sweep which the book covers) radical change in the relationship between what he calls the Oikumene—the whole community of humanity living on the Earth, and the Biosphere—the thin layer around the surface of the Earth in which life is possible. Until recent times (he is writing in the early 1970s) mankind was wholly dependent upon the Biosphere for every aspect of our physical existence. The development of civilization brought about a gradual and later an accelerating emancipation from the direct impacts of natural phenomena, at least for those human beings privileged to enjoy the fruits of technical and economic advance. However, this very 'progress' has now led to the situation where Mother Earth herself is dependent for her survival on the actions of human beings. Toynbee

---

[17] Arnold Toynbee, *Mankind and Mother Earth*, OUP, 1976.

foresees that, sooner rather than later, 'some form of unification' of the Oikumene will be necessary, if we are to avoid the matricidal and suicidal destruction of our planet's capacity to support life.

In this time of increasing individualism which was described in Chapter 1, can we imagine 'some form of unification' coming about? How might it happen? What could drive or support it? If and when environmental damage makes living conditions more and more difficult for large numbers of people, when basic resources like fresh water become increasingly scarce and contested, what can prevent a global 'war of all against all' resulting in the (temporary) survival only of the richest?

Unification of the diverse, competing and often conflicting factions in humanity can only be achieved by the recognition of something universal, something essential in every human being which is independent of race, religion, age, gender, status, wealth, politics, personality, culture or education. Fortunately, such recognition does happen, and has happened increasingly over recent centuries and decades. It has produced the concept and the ideal of universal human rights. Only this ideal, which reaches beyond everything circumstantial in human life, contains the potential to overcome the sympathies and antipathies which continually divide humanity.

Why do we believe that slavery is wrong? People did not always think so, including devout and highly moral (by the standards of their time) individuals. It was not always 'self-evident', as the US Constitution put it, that all men, let alone women, are created equal. In fact, it was not even self-evident to most of the American population at that time. What has changed? Religious texts may have been re-interpreted, but in most cases their content has not changed for many centuries. Material science has brought us ever more efficient ways of killing each other, but no proof that it is wrong to do so. If people are merely sophisticated animals, why should we not encage or slaughter them when it suits us? If human consciousness is the equivalent of a massively complex computer, what harm would there be in switching it off, or re-programming it to serve us better?

Individuality—the awareness of oneself as a separate, morally independent and unique 'I', is a precondition for consciously experiencing the unique individuality of the other. This means that, paradoxically, becoming inwardly more separate from other people increases our potential capacity truly to meet each other. The encounter between free individuals, however, is subtly but importantly different from the relationships and meetings which might previously have been shaped by the automatic sympathies and antipathies of race, family and culture. Progressive individualization and individualism has driven us further apart, but also brought the possibility of new, freer relationships, and the growing sense in a growing number of people that every individual deserves equal rights.

The recognition that another human being—every other human being—has unique value and is worthy of respect and equal treatment, is a recognition from across the Third Threshold. No other form of perception, no other source of evidence, could persuade us of this. Our feeling for the rightness of human rights is gained through our encounters with others, which carry us beyond our own souls and ultimately beyond our own partisan preferences, into a realm in which the spiritual reality of the other person becomes perceptible. When we return to ourselves, the after-image of what we have experienced stays with us. If we allow it to, it can inform our thoughts and feelings about, and actions towards, our fellow humans. Sleeping into the other person can develop into an awakening through the other, to new possibilities and higher faculties in ourselves.

I wrote this book because I believe that the understanding and experience of the social threshold, its phenomena and its challenges, will be a critical and perhaps decisive factor in the decades ahead—decades in which human relationships and the actions arising from them will have very far-reaching consequences for the long-term well-being of humanity on the Earth. To put it even more directly, unless enough of us succeed in navigating our way across the Third Threshold to a solid and reliable perception of the human spirit in other individuals, we will not be able to bring about the unification necessary to save ourselves from disaster. The crucial question is whether the still-emerging commitment to universal human rights, based not on ideology or belief but on direct inner experience, will be rapid enough, strong enough and deep enough to withstand the forces which continually seek to divide humanity.

Meeting the social threshold, finding each other across it and rediscovering ourselves, challenged and enriched, when we return, is a task and an opportunity for each of us. It cannot be delegated to markets, politicians, care agencies, religious leaders or security forces. The decisive journey starts in our own heads and hearts, and ends in our own hands.

If we omit the element of feeling from our consideration ... we discover that we can only 'contemplate' another thing or being by ceasing to *be* it and conversely that we can never 'contemplate' what in the deepest sense we are (i.e. we can never 'know ourselves'). This sounds unimpeachable. And as *tendency* it is true. In actual fact there is a force which is overcoming this tendency at every moment. All human intercourse depends on the functioning in some slight degree of this force; for without it another soul would either be so detached from me as to be undistinguishable from a lifeless object, or it would disappear into me altogether. This force is known as Love. Its whole nature is such that it enables me to become another soul *and yet* to remain separate, to go out into another being and yet remain within myself. Its whole function is to mediate between the One and the Many.

Because this force is at the core of all human conscious experience, it is impossible to speak of it. It is only possible to attempt to live it.[18]

Owen Barfield

---

[18] *Autem*, unpublished correspondance with C.S. Lewis.

Acknowledgements

Most of my learning about relationships has taken place in close communities—educational, therapeutic, residential or professional—and my warmest thanks go to those, too numerous to list here, with whom I have lived, worked, quarrelled, loved and learned, in the Camphill and Waldorf movements, in the Hoathly Hill Community, and in the Association for Social Development where I have found my closest colleagues and partners.

Some of my best teachers, inevitably, have been my children, each of whom has provided me with a rich and unique source of enlightenment.

My wife Charlene was both inspiration and collaborator, helping me to develop, deepen and enliven the content of the book. Without her challenge and support, I would have offered the reader a drier, lazier and altogether less engaging text.

Understand Your Temperament!, A Guide to the Four Temperaments
Dr Gilbert Childs

Under the Sky, Playing, Working and Enjoying Adventures in the Open Air, A Handbook for Parents, Carers and Teachers
Sally Schweizer

Well I Wonder . . . , Childhood in the Modern World, A Handbook for Parents, Carers and Teachers
Sally Schweizer

A Woman's Path, Motherhood, Love and Personal Development
Almut Bockemühl

Your Reincarnating Child, Welcoming a Soul to the World
Gilbert Childs and Sylvia Childs